Madeira

Berlitz Publishing Company, Inc.

Princeton   Mexico City   London   Eschborn   Singapore

Berlitz Trademark Reg. U.S. Patent Office and other countries
Marca Registrada

Text:	Neil Schlecht
Editor:	Media Content Marketing, Inc.
Photography:	Neil Schlecht except pages 4, 5, 26, 50 (left), 51 (right), 56, 61, 64, 67, 68, 77, 80, 89, 90, 94 by Paul Murphy
Cover Photo:	Paul Murphy
Photo Editor:	Naomi Zinn
Layout:	Media Content Marketing, Inc.
Cartography:	Raffaele De Gennaro

*Although the publisher tries to insure the accuracy of all the infor-
mation in this book, changes are inevitable and errors may result.
The publisher cannot be responsible for any resulting loss, incon-
venience, or injury. If you find an error in this guide, please let the
editors know by writing to Berlitz Publishing Company, 400
Alexander Park, Princeton, NJ 08540-6306.*

ISBN 2-8315-7699-7

Printed in Italy
010/102 RE

CONTENTS

- A  in the text denotes a highly recommended sight

Madeira

MADEIRA AND THE MADEIRANS

A mere speck in the middle of the Atlantic Ocean, Madeira has all the elements of a mysterious dream world. The volcanic island is thickly draped with vegetation, a colorful riot of flowers and fruit trees. Rugged mountains peek through the clouds, and microclimates hover over isolated villages. Spectacular cliffs crash hundreds of feet below to the deep blue surf.

Even though foreign invaders stormed Portugal around 2000 B.C., Madeira was discovered only a few decades before Columbus made his way to America. Though part of the Portuguese empire since the great expedition teams of the 15th century claimed it for King João I, Madeira is nearer to Africa than Lisbon. It lies 600 km (375 miles) off the coast of Morocco and nearly 1,000 km (600 miles) southwest of the Portuguese capital.

Formed from volcanic eruptions many millions of years ago, Madeira, like the Canary Islands, is an archipelago. The land is like an iceberg; massive mountains poke through the clouds, forming the mere tip of a submerged mass. Only one other island in the small group is inhabited — the little known, arid, and much flatter holiday hideaway of Porto Santo. Christopher Columbus visited Porto Santo in the second half of the 15th century, marrying the local governor's daughter.

Few places on earth can rival Madeira's wealth of natural gifts, especially in so small an area. The island is blanketed with flowers: birds of paradise, their beak-like flowers bright orange, blossom in open fields. Fragrant hydrangeas line walking paths skirting the edges of mountain terraces. Private and public gardens burst with orchids, bougainvillea, and jacarandas, while orchards heave with mangoes, passion fruit, watermelons, and avocados.

In the mountains, water streams down from unseen springs: a one-hour walk might take you past half a dozen waterfalls. The cold waters around the island, once prime whaling territory, are today a marine sanctuary for whales, dolphins, and seals. And all of this in year-round sub-tropical spring weather with a southerly breeze and temperatures averaging 22° C in summer and 17° C in winter.

Madeira seems much larger than its diminutive size, just 57 km (35 miles) long and 22 km (13 miles) wide. The terrain is so mountainous, and its roads so tortuous, that distances are magnified in terms of both time and effort. This can breed insularity; some villagers have never been as far as Funchal and the thought of making the long trip to the mainland is even more remote. Yet young and upwardly mobile islanders do go off in search of fortune, and the most successful return from Brazil, Venezuela, or South Africa to build sumptuous villas overlooking the Bay of Funchal.

Madeira, alas, is no simple portrait of a Gauguin-like tropical paradise. With a history of emigration and return, of welcoming visiting merchants and seafarers, and, during a brief period of occupation, a garrison of British troops, islanders are a cosmopolitan mix. The populace is an engaging stew of dark North African complexions and blonde, blue-eyed northern Europeans.

Funchal, the island's capital, major harbor, and only city of any note, merely hints at Madeira's riches. The capital's white houses and tile roofs are clustered on picturesque hills sloping down to a steep bay, which makes for a pretty picture. The city is undeniably pleasant, but its noise and traffic don't seem so far removed from the more conveniently located places most people come here to avoid. Almost half of

Madeira's 270,000 people live in Funchal (pronounced "foon-*shawl*"), and cruise-ship passengers stride ashore daily for a frenzied flurry of sightseeing and shopping. Other visitors kick back in luxury hotels crowding the city's western seafront. In recent years a gleaming new high-rise *zona turista*

Desertas and Selvagens

In addition to the two inhabited islands, Madeira and Porto Santo, the archipelago comprises another five islands and numerous minor rocks and reefs, all of which once constituted part of a land mass that also included the Canary Islands and the Azores. The islands fall into two groups: the Ilhas Desertas (desert islands) and Ilhas Selvagens (wild or savage islands). The former consist of three islands, the nearest being 12 km (19 miles) southeast of Madeira. However, these desert islands are far from the Robinson Crusoe idyll; they are barren and inhospitable to the point where, aside from the occasional goat and rabbit, the most notable land creature is a large, poisonous black spider.

The sea life around the islands is a different story, however. Dolphins and turtles are occasionally spotted, and there is a colony of monk seals. Birdwatchers will relish the opportunity to see shearwaters and petrels. Marine biologists and nature conservationists are the only regular human visitors, for even though excursion boats frequently make trips to these isles in summer, landing is restricted to authorized persons only.

Meanwhile, the two Selvagens Islands, usually known as Grande (large) and Pequena (small), are Madeiran only in name (they are actually closer to Tenerife, of the Canary Islands), and lie 285 km (177 miles) to the south. Like the Desertas, they are uninhabited and devoted entirely to nature conservation.

Women selling flowers in Funchal often dress in the traditionally colorful way.

has sprung up to confront the old-world hotels and distinguished *quintas* (rural estates) of Madeira's more peaceful past.

Funchal is less the sum of Madeira, though, than a gateway to the rest of the island, whose real charms begin in the hillsides just a few minutes outside of town. Spectacular gardens, like the Botanic Garden and Quinta do Palheiro, are only a short bus or taxi ride from the capital.

Small-scale agriculture dominates the island's landscape, employing about a fifth of the people. Depending on the altitude and whether you happen to be on the warm south coast or the marginally cooler north coast, you will see terraces of bananas and vines that produce the grapes for fortified Madeira wine. There are windswept mountain peaks, craggy cliffs that plummet to the sea, and emerald valleys that could be stand-ins for Ireland or Scotland. From strategically situated lookout points (*miradouros*) you can take in these magical panoramas and look down upon villages carved out of the mountains, at least one so isolated it only began to receive TV signals in the late 1980s.

Driving a car along the hairpin curves on mountain roads and coastal lanes, getting sprayed by waterfalls and constantly rewarded with spectacular vistas can be an exhilarating experience, but Madeira is best viewed by getting out of the car or bus and exploring on two feet. The island is heaven for anyone who enjoys being outside, whether your taste runs to gentle walks or hardcore hiking. Madeira's system of irrigation channels, known as *levadas*, carries water down from the mountains on gentle gradients and provides a ready-made system of trails. The canals — more than 1,300 miles of them crisscross the island — have level footpaths running along their entire length. Walkers of all ages and abilities need only find a levada to take in some of the finest countryside anywhere. Several of these walks, which will be discussed in this book, are among the highlights of Madeira.

With such rapturous scenery and a climate that is consistently delightful, perhaps it would be unfair to expect nature to have bestowed the island with miles of perfect sands as well. Madeira has no beaches to speak of — though the day when an enterprising hotel builds its own man-made beach can't be too far off. In the meantime, if a lounge chair by the pool just can't compare, you'll have to follow in the wake of Columbus and dock on the neighboring island of Porto Santo, a popular day trip.

The only other inhabited island in the archipelago, Porto Santo has a 9-km-long beach running the length of its south coast, but few other attractions. While some surely would find the notion of an island vacation with no beach time an unusual prospect indeed, perhaps it isn't at all a tragedy that Madeira's shoreline crashes so violently into the ocean. A Madeira with sandy beaches and direct flights from Great Britain and other points in Europe (and beginning in late 2000, North America) would surely not have been capable of staving off the mass-tourist market as it has thus far. Lack of sand has kept Madeira from modeling itself after Mallorca.

For decades, Madeira has instead attracted a genteel, even anachronistic form of island tourism. Afternoon tea and black-tie dinners are still served at the most elegant hotels. The typical visitor is still older and wealthier than in most holiday destinations, but times are beginning to change — as they are across Portugal, no longer the forgotten backwater of Europe. Funchal's new tourist zone testifies to local travel industry ambitions. Today Madeira is being discovered by younger travelers who might also indulge in the spas and dining that world-class hotels offer, but are just as likely to seek out the modest inns up in the mountains and strap on their boots for serious hiking.

Madeirans, like most Portuguese, are a generally quiet and reserved people. Add to this geographical isolation and the difficulties for most of a harsh agricultural existence (where few have the machinery to help in the tiny terraced fields), and you might forgive the islanders if they seemed less than welcoming.

Instead you will find friendly people who, in spite of a 12-month season that for decades has deposited tourists from wealthier nations on their shores, are refreshingly hospitable. They are proud of the scenic beauty, delectable wines, and exquisite hand embroidery that their tiny island has become rightly famous for.

The tourism ante is being upped by hoteliers, entrepreneurs, and government officials eager to broaden Madeira's offerings and appeal. But the allure of Madeira remains its absence of man-made attractions and abundance of natural ones. Some people still suggest that Madeira is part of the lost continent of Atlantis, and though it has become easier and easier to get there, the island still seems otherworldly.

A BRIEF HISTORY

B efitting a lush, tropical island stranded in the middle of the ocean, Madeira's origins are shrouded in mystery and fanciful legend. Some claim that the archipelago is what remains of Plato's lost Atlantis, or part of a landmass that once fused the continents of Europe and America.

The Portuguese Step Ashore

Recorded history of the volcanic archipelago begins in relatively recent times: 1418, just as the golden age of Portuguese discovery was erupting. Under the leadership of Henry the Navigator, caravels set out from the westernmost point of the Algarve, in southern Portugal, in search of foreign lands, fame, and wealth. João Gonçalves Zarco, sailing in the service of Prince Henry, made the first of many famous Portuguese discoveries, which would culminate a century later in Magellan's historic circumnavigation of the globe. Zarco happened upon a small volcanic archipelago 1,000 km from Lisbon.

Perhaps Zarco knew precisely where he was heading, having learned of the existence of Madeira from a Castilian source. After all, the waters of the Canary Islands, only 445 km (275 miles) to the south, had occupied busy shipping lanes for very nearly a century, and Genovese maps from the mid-14th century depict both Madeira and Porto Santo.

More likely, Zarco was heading for Guinea and storms forced him onto the beach of Porto Santo. If so, then he was extremely fortunate, for he managed to land on the only large, sandy beach for hundreds of miles around. Little wonder he subsequently named it Porto Santo (Holy Port).

The following year Zarco returned to claim the larger island he had seen from Porto Santo, and with him went

Tristão Vaz Teixeira and Bartolomeu Perestrelo. They officially became the first men to set foot on the heavily forested island, naming it *Ilha da Madeira*, "Island of Timber." The Portuguese Crown, delighted with its first important discovery, immediately embarked on a program of colonization. Zarco and Teixeira were appointed co-governors of Madeira, while Perestrelo was awarded Porto Santo.

Starting from Scratch

Whoever first stepped ashore on Madeira discovered no signs of previous habitation — no Stone-Age natives, as the Spanish found on the Canary Islands, and no mysterious monuments to the past, as on the Balearics.

Occupation of Madeira began in the early 1420s as a decidedly minimalist project: colonists arrived with only as much as they could carry from mainland Portugal. They found plenty of water pouring down from the mountains, and more timber than anyone knew what to do with. So they set about clearing the land for agriculture, setting fire to massive tracts of forest. Legend says that a great fire burned for seven years on the island, leveling it of all its trees. The fire provided the soil with a rich ash fertilizer, which complemented the luxuriant growing conditions of tropical sun and plentiful water.

The Portuguese saw valuable economic opportunity in their new possession and ordered Malvasia grapes from Crete and sugar cane from Italy in an effort to seed the island's first cash crops. The project was not a simple one. Colonists had to locate enough level ground to grow crops on and solve the issue of irrigating them. Brute strength, without aid of machinery, carved flat surfaces out of the mountains, and settlers built the terraces — still seen today — on the steep slopes.

The problem of watering crops was solved by the irrigation system known as *levadas* — simply-designed water channels that wound down from water sources on the verdant mountain tops. The levadas were largely built by slave laborers from Africa, whose primary employment was on sugar plantations. New Madeirans traded sugar, the era's dominant luxury item, with Britain and Flanders, and they proved skillful in the art of winemaking. The island's burgeoning economic significance propelled population growth, and by the middle of the 15th century Madeira was home to 800 families. A 1514 census recorded 5,000 inhabitants.

In 1478 Madeira welcomed a visitor who would greatly assist the island's future wine trade. Christopher Columbus, not yet a sailor of any renown, sailed to Madeira on an assignment to buy sugar cane. His sojourn was unsuccessful, as money failed to arrive for part of the shipment. Yet Columbus (Columbo in Portuguese) returned six years later, by which time evidence suggests that he had become an experienced sugarcane merchant. His later discovery of the New World brought prosperity to the Madeiran economy: the island's strategic location on the great East-West trading

Sé, Funchal's cathedral, dates all the way back to Madeira's early days.

route meant that ships anchored and took on food, water, and the valuable trading commodity of Madeira wine.

Columbus had his eye on more than sugar in Madeira. He married Dona Filipa Moniz (Perestrelo), the daughter of Porto Santo's first governor, and lived on the island for a period, fathering a son there. Even today, there are those on Porto Santo who will tell you that it was due to his time spent there that Christopher Columbus learned navigation techniques and the ways of the ocean, and found the inspiration to undertake his voyage of 1492.

Invaders

In 1566 Madeira suffered its worst disaster. Well aware of the island's burgeoning wealth and repository of supplies, the French pirate Bertrand de Montluc sailed into Funchal harbor with his 11-galleon armada and 1,300 men. He unleashed a 16-day reign of terror that left 300 Madeirans dead, stocks of sugar destroyed, and the island plundered. By the time Lisbon mounted a rescue mission, the pirates had long fled (though Montluc himself had been killed during the raid). As a result of the attack, Porto Santo, which had also been scourged by these villains of the seas, went on to build castles and early warning systems, which allowed the citizens to defend themselves or flee if necessary. On the mainland, an invasion of even greater significance followed in 1580, when Philip II of Spain proclaimed himself king of Portugal and marched his armies across the border. The Spanish remained for another 60 years, and Madeira became a Spanish territory.

In the 16th century, Madeira surrendered its dominance of the sugarcane industry to another, much larger, Portuguese colony, Brazil. Sugar cane had taken a hefty toll on the Madeiran soil; exhausted plantations were supplanted by less-demanding grape vines. Although sugarcane continues to be grown today (for molasses and the brandy-like *aguardente*), it has long ceased to be the island's major crop.

The British Are Coming!

Britain's political and economic connections to Madeira can be traced to the 17th century. In 1662 Charles II married Portugal's Catherine of Bragança. A provision written into the bride's dowry granted special favors to British settlers on Madeira; had Charles been more aggressive still, perhaps the Portuguese would have agreed to hand over the island to Britain in its entirety.

First Man on Madeira?

Some say that the first man on Madeira was not the Portuguese adventurer João Gonçalves Zarco but an Englishman named Robert Machim (sometimes written Machin).

One version of the story is that Machim was a knight at the court of Edward III and sought to marry above his class, to a girl named Anne d'Arfet (or Anne of Hertford). The determined young lovers boarded a France-bound ship, which was thrown severely off course. The pair ended up shipwrecked on Madeira. The lady died of exposure soon afterwards and Machim buried her by the bay where they had come ashore. Machim too died (it is said of a broken heart) and was buried alongside her by members of the same shipwrecked crew, who eventually escaped on a log raft and recounted the tragic tale.

Zarco, who is much more widely credited with the discovery of Madeira, was aware of the legend. He is said to have found the grave of the couple, naming the site Machico in honor of Machin. The couple's resting place is said to be beneath the chapel of Senhor dos Milagres on the eastern side of Machico Bay.

Both Madeira and Britain benefited from a new regulation that governed the shipment of Madeira wine and made it the only wine that could be exported directly to the British possessions in the Western hemisphere (providing, of course, it was carried by a British vessel). All other wines had to be shipped to the Americas via a British harbor. Such trading rights attracted more Britons to the island, who founded dynastic families that in some cases still constitute the island's economic elite. Wine profits were huge, and by 1800 exports had reached nine million bottles per year. Many of the grand country *quintas* (villas) that still dot the island today have their roots in the early Madeira wine industry.

British troops arrived on the island in 1801 to protect against possible invasion by the French, but they were with-

The Bay of Machico, Madeira's first settlement, is made beautiful by a combination of mountains, water, and sky.

drawn following the Treaty of Amiens in 1802. In 1807 the Treaty was put in jeopardy and the troops returned, remaining until 1814. Many of the garrison remained and settled permanently on the island.

War and Pestilence

The second half of the 19th century on Madeira was plagued by natural disaster. In 1852 the island's precious vines were blighted by mildew, wiping out an estimated 90 percent of the total crop. Just four years later, cholera claimed the lives of up to 7,000 Madeirans, and in 1873 the dreaded disease phylloxera destroyed the remainder of the vineyards. Potato and sugar crops were also badly affected during this period.

Portugal took up arms during World War I, siding with the British and French. Madeira's strategic position for Atlantic shipping did not escape the notice of the German High Command, and in December of that year a German submarine bombarded the Funchal harbor and sank three French ships.

Modern Times

As mainland Portugal lurched into a political and economic crisis that would bring down the country's republican government, many miles away Madeira was busy looking after distinguished visitors and its developing tourist trade. In fact, Madeira had been a sought-after destination since the middle of the 19th century, attracting wealthy British sun-lovers, minor royalty, and aristocrats from many countries. The celebrated Reid's Hotel had opened its doors in 1890, and seaplane service started operating from Lisbon in 1921. Madeira was awarded further cachet when the last of the Austro-Hungarian emperors, Charles I of Austria (also Charles IV of Hungary), chose Madeira as his home in exile after the war.

In 1932 Portugal gained a new ruler and dictator, ex-Minister of Finance Dr. António Salazar. Following a bloodless coup in 1974 called the "Carnation Revolution," Salazar's successor, Dr. Marcelo Caetano, was overthrown and free elections were held. Madeira was then granted autonomy, in addition to the right to determine its own taxes and send a deputation to the Portuguese government.

In 1986 Portugal joined the European Economic Community (now the European Union, or EU). Funding from the EU has been heavily invested in the island's infrastructure and fishing industry. The nonstop construction of roads and tunnels and the massive expansion of the Funchal airport seem to indicate that Madeira plans to see the tiny island accommodate as many people as possible. For several decades tourism has dominated the island's economy, but Madeira's enduring appeal lies in preserving it as a sublime tropical retreat far removed from the rest of the world.

Celebrated Stopovers

Madeira has welcomed many distinguished sea voyagers in its long tradition of hospitality, including, in 1815, the defeated Napoleon Bonaparte. En route to exile on St. Helena in the South Atlantic, Napoleon's ship anchored to take on supplies. The only visitor allowed aboard was the British consul, who graciously presented Britain's old enemy with bottles of vintage Madeira wine to help wile away his confinement. (Napoleon responded with gold coins.)

History just about repeated itself after the 1974 coup, when the deposed Portuguese leaders — ex-President Tomás and Prime Minister Caetano — also stopped at Madeira en route to exile in Brazil. This time, however, the defeated party was allowed ashore, but only to be locked up in the São Lourenço fortress.

WHERE TO GO

Madeira's small size can be deceiving. At just 57 km (35 miles) long by 22 km (13 miles) wide, first glance might indicate that two days would be sufficient to see the whole place. Even in a rental car, Madeira's steep, mountainous terrain and winding, two-lane roads make that very difficult. The coastal route is beautiful, but potentially nerve-wracking; only the southern section from Caniço west to Ribeira Brava is served by the excellent highway (*via rápida*) cut through the mountains.

A minimum of three days is necessary to see a good portion of the island; a week allows a visitor to do it justice and take the time to enjoy its scenic outdoors at a relaxed pace. Until recently, most visitors — counseled not to attempt to drive the island's difficult roads — hopped aboard bus daytrips that took in the main attractions. Roads are improving, though, and while driving isn't necessarily the horror it once was, traveling by rental car should be reserved for confident drivers comfortable on steep, winding terrain.

More and more visitors are choosing to stay outside of Funchal; the offer of mountain lodges and smaller coastal hotels has greatly improved over the years, and there are now visitors who barely set foot in the capital.

FUNCHAL

Funchal is the single town of any size on the island, indeed in the whole of the archipelago. Most historic buildings, museums, and traditional sights are located in the capital. With a population of 120,000, it is a larger city than most expect to find on such a tiny island, but in fact you can walk across the center in just 10 to 15 minutes. Exploring inland to the north is difficult on foot, however: The streets become very steep.

Get your fill of cacti in the succulent section of the Jardim Botânico.

Nevertheless, walking remains the only practical way to see Funchal: The narrow, cobbled streets were never meant for motor vehicles, and they can be surprisingly congested with traffic.

One way to get your bearings upon arrival is to walk out on the jetty known as the **Ilhéu de Pontinha** and view Funchal as those aboard cruise ships do. Built in 1962, the Pontinha tunnels its way straight through the middle of the old fortress, which until then was perched on top of a tiny island known as Looe Rock.

Funchal's deep natural harbor propelled the city's development in the 15th and 16th centuries, when Madeira became known to expeditions on their way to the Far East and Americas. With the exception of ocean liners and picturesque fishing boats, Funchal remains a working port (handling containerized freight) and home to a small oil terminal.

The view of the town from the harbor is outstanding: Squat white houses with red terracotta roofs climb steeply through tropical greenery all around the spacious bay.

Madeira's rugged mountains form an attractive backdrop to the city. Just north is the town of Monte, and tucked into the hills north and east of Funchal are two of the city's best gardens, the Jardim Botânico and Quinta do Palheiro. The newest hotel zone is due west of the city along the coast, stretching for 5 km (3 miles) or so before the coast bends on the way to the small town, Câmara de Lobos, and the high cliff, Cabo Girão.

The Center of Town

The dominant building on the seafront is the **Palácio de São Lourenço** (Fortress of St. Lawrence). Erected in the 16th century, it guarded the bay against pirate ships — you can still see the ancient cannons poking through the crenellated walls. White-gloved sentries guard the main gate of the fort, now the residence of Madeira's military governors. Although the main building is not open to the public, the official residence of the Portuguese government may be visited by prearranged, guided tours (Tel. 291/20 25 30).

At the intersection of Avenida Zarco and the main drag, Avenida Arriaga, stands a statue of Madeira's discoverer, João Gonçalves Zarco — often referred to as the "First Captain." The imposing **Palácio do Governo Regional**, a handsome building with tiled patios and the administrative headquarters of Madeira, rises behind the Zarco monument to the right.

The Palacio do Governo Regional is a defining aspect of central Funchal.

Av. Arriaga is particularly pretty during late spring, when jacaranda trees are in full blossom. Along here you will find the tourist information office and, just next door, at no. 28, the **Adegas de São Francisco** (the Old Blandy Wine Lodge), the oldest working wine lodge in Madeira. The atmospheric place was part of a Franciscan monastery built in the 17th century. Although Madeira's fortified wines aren't made here any longer, you can take a tour of the lodge (Mon–Fri, 10:30 am and 3:30pm, Sat 11am) and the wine cellars. A tour isn't necessary to visit (and have a taste or make a purchase) at the handsome vintage cellar and tasting room.

A few steps west of the lodge is the small but lush **Parque da Cidade** (City Park), a delightful urban green space. Exotic trees and flowers are mingled with statuary, and black swans glide across a small pond. Across from the park is the **Teatro Municipal** (Municipal Theater), a miniature Victorian gem that hosts periodic concerts, while opposite the wine lodge is an old Scottish kirk (church), another indicator of the strong British influence on the island's development.

Across the street is the incongruous but elegant **Toyota Automobile Showroom,** once the Chamber of Commerce and worth noting for its fine blue-and-white *azulejo* (tile) vignettes that depict scenes from old Madeira.

Toward the center of town, at the end of Av. Arriaga (at Rua João Tavira) is Funchal's principal landmark, the **Sé** (cathedral). Begun at the end of the 15th century, Funchal's Sé is one of the city's only surviving buildings from the early days of colonization. The exterior is adorned with a brick clock tower, but the cathedral's interior is considerably more impressive. It has Gothic arches, a splendid inlaid cedar ceiling of Moorish design, beautifully carved blue-and-gold choir stalls, gilded altars, and a sprinkling of nice *azulejos* (blue-and-white ceramic tiles).

Funchal's main square, Praça do Município, is lined on one side by the Câmara Municipal, or town hall.

A walk along Rua do Aljube takes you to some of Funchal's pedestrian shopping streets. Tucked behind Rua João Tavira and Rua da Carreira is **Praça do Município**, the town's dignified main square, with a mosaic of black-and-white stones and pretty white buildings on three sides. To the left is the 17th-century **Igreja do Colégio** (Collegiate Church), originally founded by the Jesuits in 1574. A spacious and airy old place, it's decorated with 17th- and 18th-century tiles, paintings, and gilt-wood carving. The adjacent school served as a barracks for British troops in the 19th century.

Straight ahead on the square stands the **Câmara Municipal** (Town Hall), which occupies a former 18th-century palace. Don't miss the graceful, 19th-century statue of *Leda and the Swan* in the inner courtyard. The statue used to be in the old fish market — a fact corroborated by the tile panel outside the present municipal market (see page 29).

On the square's third (south) side is the very interesting **Museu de Arte Sacra** (Museum of Sacred Art), housed in what was a 17th-century palace, formerly the Bishop of Funchal's residence. The outstanding works on view include a dozen or so 15th- and 16th-century Flemish paintings, regarded as some of the richest in Portugal and rare even in the rest of Europe. These vibrant masterpieces, as well as other excellent works from the Portuguese school of the same period, belonged to Funchal's wealthy sugar merchants, who during the 16th century traded their "white gold" for principal art treasures of the day.

The back door of the museum leads to Rua do Bispo (Street of the Bishop), and both this and the parallel street, Rua Queimada Cima, are worth exploring. Then continue west from the Praça do Municipio on Rua da Carreira, a bustling street full of interesting, old-fashioned shops and buildings. It is particularly noteworthy for the cheap restaurants that cater primarily to city workers, but also satisfy a good number of tourists.

One of many treasures at the Museu de Arte Sacra is this Flemish St. Peter.

A few yards left is the **Museu Vicente de Fotografia** (Vicente Photography Museum). It is easy to miss, but once you have spotted it, cross the street and look back at the faded, ancient sign and the colonnades on the wall above. The narrow entrance squeezes past a bookshop and opens out into a delightful, plant-filled patio. This was the first public photo studio opened in Portugal (during the 1850s), and some of the props on display are amusingly quaint. In addition to the varied selection of memorabilia and antique photographic equipment, don't miss having a flick through the albums of photographs of old Madeira, dating from 1884.

Just a couple of hundred yards north of the São Francisco gardens, the streets rise sharply. Off Rua da Carreira is Calçada Santa Clara, a picturesque, hilly street full of interest. At the junction with Rua Mouraria is the **Museu Municipal do Funchal** (Municipal Museum), yet another 18th-century aristocratic home converted into a museum (entrance on Rua Mouraria). On the ground floor is a modest aquarium showing the sealife of Madeira, while upstairs is a thoroughly old-fashioned collection of stuffed local sea and land creatures. The museum is probably best for younger children.

Returning to the hill, on the opposite side of the museum is the charming **Igreja de São Pedro,** an unusual church. Its walls are lined entirely with blue-and-white checked-pattern *azulejos* and it has a beautifully painted wood ceiling, 10 chandeliers, and a massively gilded altar and side chapels.

A few yards farther up the hill is the recently restored **Casa Museu Frederico de Freitas**. The private collection includes paintings of old Madeira by 19th-century English artists and the apartments of a well-to-do 18th-century Madeiran household.

Continue uphill to the **Convento de Santa Clara**. Built toward the end of the 15th century and expanded two centuries later, it's now a school run by Franciscan nuns. The convent church is a splendid building, with walls completely covered by rare, 17th-century *azulejos* in geometric patterns, and with a fine painted ceiling. Madeira's discoverer, Zarco, is buried beneath the altar, but the memorial to him vanished long ago. The tomb at the back of the church is not Zarco's, but that of family members.

During his stint as governor of the island, Zarco is believed to have lived a short distance up Calçada do Pico, in the **Quinta das Cruzes**. Originally constructed in the 15th century, but rebuilt after an earthquake in 1748 and expanded in the 19th century, this is Funchal's finest *quinta* (estate villa) open to the public. The main house is now a museum of antiques, including furniture from a variety of centuries and origins. There are superb 16th-century Indo-Portuguese and 17th-century Madeiran as well as 18th- and 19th-century English pieces.

The house is surrounded by a lovely, somewhat unkempt garden of exotic flowers, trees, and plants (including a good orchid section). However, the outstanding feature is the "archaeological garden," an outdoor display of relics from some of the oldest places on the island — tombstones, pieces taken from important buildings, and two splendid early-16th-century stone Manueline windows (pick up the Quinta's own leaflet for information on these).

The road separating Quinta das Cruzes from the Convento leads to a lookout point with a view over the town, the port, and the dome of the English Church.

The Market, Old Town, and Seafront

Between two streams — *ribeiras* (riverbeds) that carry excess water down from the mountains to the sea — is Rua Dr. Fernão Ornelas, a street lined with old shops that leads to

Funchal's central market. In spring, the little rivers are hidden beneath trellises of blazing bougainvillea.

Directly ahead lies the **Mercado dos Lavradores**  (Workers' Market), housed in a two-story, open-roofed structure built in 1941. The market is open from Monday to Saturday from early in the morning until late afternoon; the best time to visit is on a Friday or Saturday, when fishermen, farmers, and traders from all over the island pour into town. This is the only time when the central part is filled with stalls.

The market is bustling, fragrant, and colorful, with exotic fruits, vegetables, and fish of all shapes, colors, and sizes. Meat stalls can be found around the outside, as well as several wicker and handicraft shops. You will also find an open-air fruit, vegetable, and clothes market just behind the main market, in the park area next to the bus stops.

Mercado dos Lavradores is the beginning of the **Old Town** quarter (even though you will not see signs for the *Zona Velha* until farther east). The main streets are the narrow, cobbled alleyway of Rua de Santa Maria and, parallel, Rua Dom Carlos I. This east end of Funchal is the antithesis of the opulent hotel zone to the west: It is poor and decaying, but filled with character.

Visitors are attracted to the Mercado dos Lavradores by sight and smell.

The only visible gentrification is the row of restaurants that you reach at the pedestrian-only stretch leading to the **Capela do Corpo Santo** (Chapel of the Body of Christ). The chapel, dating to the end of the 15th century, is the oldest in Funchal. Although a few artisan's workshops are nearby, this old fishermen's quarter is mainly a residential area.

Down a narrow alleyway, past Edwardian-style beach huts used by local fishermen for storage and napping in, is the 17th-century **Forte de São Tiago** (St. James Fortress). Built in the 17th century and expanded in the mid-1700s, the picturesque fort now houses a modest **Museu de Arte Contemporánea** (Museum of Contemporary Art). Another sign that this part of Funchal is being revitalized is the new lido, known as Barreirinha, on the beach below the **Igreja de Santa Maria Maior,** an elegant 18th-century church worth a visit. The terrace of the café below has fine views of the sea to the east.

Along the seafront, just off Rua da Alfândaga, is the **Parlamento Regional** (Regional Parliament Building). Built in the 16th century and formerly the Old Customs House (Alfândega Velha), the oldest parts of this building lie inside the imposing gateway. The stone-paved lobby area is dominated by an enormous Egyptian-style vase, which at over 5 m ($17^1/_2$ ft) tall, stands almost as high as a giraffe. Made recently by a team of Portuguese and Brazilian craftsmen, it is listed in the *Guinness Book of Records* as the world's tallest ceramic vase.

West of Town

Avenida Arriaga ends at the Praça do Infante, where a statue of Prince Henry the Navigator (a copy of the one at Lagos in the Algarve) sits at the easternmost tip of **Parque Santa Catarina** (St. Catherine Park). A delightful hilltop retreat, it

*The Municipal Gardens at the end of Avenida Arriaga
provide a pleasantly pastoral sanctuary.*

has splendid views over the Marina to the bay beyond. Aside from the gardens, lake, and playground, other points of interest include a statue of Christopher Columbus (who may have lived in Funchal for a while), and, close by, the Chapel of Santa Catarina, dating from the 17th century. At the west end of the park, the elegant pink **Quinta Vigia** is the residence of Madeira's governor. The well-tended gardens are open to the public, as is the chapel.

Above the park looms the startling sight of the Pestana Carlton Park Hotel (designed by Oscar Niemeyer, famous for the futuristic Brasilia). The giant box of a hotel signals the start of the traditional hotel zone, flush with well-known, deluxe 5-star hotels such as the Savoy, the Madeira Carlton, and Reid's, plus a few 4-star hotels, *quintas,* and posh restaurants.

Just north of Avenida do Infante (along Rua Dr. Pita) is the delightful **Quinta Magnólia** park. Here you can swim or play tennis in the morning, have a walk around the gardens, and round off the afternoon with tea on the patio.

Beginning west of Reid's Hotel is the newest hotel zone, known as the *Zona Turista* (Tourist Zone). The enclave, which in its entirety exists to host and serve visitors, is perennially stocked with cranes, as new hotels and restaurants continue to be erected.

Glorious Gardens

A short bus or taxi ride into the steep hillsides northeast of Funchal (on the road to Camacha) leads to the **Jardim Botânico** (Botanical Garden), the island's most comprehensive public garden. Inaugurated in 1960, the gardens have exam-

The Jardim Botânico recently commemorated 40 years of Madeiran flora with this beautiful display.

ples of virtually every plant that grows on Madeira and lots of subtropical flowers and plants from places like South Africa and Brazil. It occupies steep terraces that offer fine views over Funchal. The adjacent **Parque do Loiro** (Tropical Bird Park) has been incorporated into the Botanic Garden. In open areas and cages, it has all manner of birds, parrots, and peacocks.

Just a short walk down the hill is the **Jardim Orquídea** (Pregetter's Orchid Garden). A relatively new project in orchid breeding, it has some 50,000 plants and more than 4,000 varieties of delicate orchids.

Another of Funchal's loveliest gardens, five minutes away by car is **Quinta da Boa Vista** (Rua Luis Figueiroa de Albuquerque). The lovely 200-year old house and garden are flush with orchids. The cymbidiums have received many awards, most notably from the British Royal Horticultural Society. Orchids are also on sale here, and you will never find them any fresher. The grounds include an ancient wine press and a charming thatched cottage.

The most splendid of Madeira's horticultural wonders, however, are the gardens at **Quinta do Palheiro Ferreiro** (formerly called the Blandy Gardens). The hillside estate, only a short bus ride from Funchal, is the property of the family that owned Reid's Hotel and is one of the famous producers of Madeira wine. The original *quinta* and chapel of the Count of Carvalhal, Quinta do Palheiro has been in the hands of the Blandy family for more than a century. (The main house is closed to the public.)

> Taxi fares to tourist spots outside the center of Funchal — to the Botanic Garden, Monte, or Quinta do Palheiro — are *tarifas fixas* (set fares). The meter is not turned on, and the passenger is charged a standard 3,000 esc., or $15, roundtrip. City buses 31 (Jardim Botânico), 36 (Qunita do Palheiro), 20, and 21 (Monte) also serve these attractions.

The gardens, designed by an 18th-century French architect and established over several generations, are most famous for their camellias, though the diversity of exotic plants, including a lush array of tropical species, is quite remarkable. The long, cobbled entrance avenue is shaded by plane trees, while the fields which lie on each side are carpeted with a wonderful spread of agapanthus and arum, and belladonna lilies in season.

Formal and informal areas are landscaped with pools and fountains, while terraces tumble down the hillsides. A deep, wild ravine with thick tropical vegetation is nicknamed the "River of Hell." Yet the garden retains the distinctive charming and peaceful atmosphere of the timeless grounds of an English country house.

Many find that the carrinho, a variation on the toboggan, is a charming way to get around the island.

AROUND FUNCHAL

A number of excellent visits are within easy reach of Funchal. Tour operators often promote Monte, Pico dos Barcelos, and Curral das Freiras as a popular half-day excursion.

Monte has been a fashionable hilltop town ever since wealthy merchants and exiled European aristocrats in the 19th century built their splendid *quintas* up here in the cool air above Funchal. Today it's perhaps best known for the anachronistic toboggan rides that originate here. The main square in Monte pleasantly evokes yesteryear. The rack-and-pinion railway that once labored up the ferociously steep hill closed in the 1930s, but the railway station is still here, its arches visible over the perfectly clipped public gardens **Jardim do Monte** (established 1894). In fact, in 1930, after 37 years of service, the train exploded, killing a number of people. By the advent of World War II, Monte's golden age was over.

A short walk along a path from the square is the elegant and richly decorated **Igreja de Nossa Senhora do Monte** (Our Lady of Monte), dedicated to Madeira's patron saint. On 15 August, thousands of locals make the annual pilgrimage to the church. A chapel on the left holds the tomb of the last of the Austro-Hungarian emperors, Charles I of Austria (and IV of Hungary), who died on Madeira in 1922. At the bottom of the church is the starting point for the island's best-known attraction, the **Carrinhos de Monte** — the unique roller-coaster ride down the hill aboard a wicker toboggan (see page 36).

The **Jardim do Palácio do Monte** (Monte Palace Tropical Gardens), a short walk east of the church, is firmly rooted in the past. The gardens that surround the château-like Monte Palace — once the area's most fashionable hotels — are home to hundreds of plants and various other displays. The entrance fee is quite high by Madeiran standards (1,500 esc.), but within the gates is an impressive collection of native and exotic flora (especially good cycads), a koi pond, porcelain collection, and historical artifacts from throughout Portugal, including architectural pieces taken from important buildings

Downhill Racers

Monte's famous wicker toboggans were originally used at the beginning of the 19th century to carry freight down the frighteningly steep 5-km (3-mile) hill between Monte and Funchal. It is said that a British merchant, living in Monte and weary of winding his way down to Funchal every day, hit on the idea that the same toboggans could carry people. A wicker seat was fixed to the basic sled and so the *carrinho de cesto* (literally "basket-car") was born.

Each *carrinho* is controlled by two white-attired *condutores*, complete with traditional straw hats, who give an initial push and then ride along until another push, or pull, or sudden brake, is required, depending upon the desired speed and any traffic ahead. They stop, by the way, like Fred Flintstone might if he wore shoes: with the rubber soles of their simple boots. The toboggan rides have long been popular with visitors; many a cruise-ship passenger has been whisked up to Monte to make the journey, before disappearing almost straight back to sea.

Alas, the current toboggan ride is a pale shadow of its former self (even though the price charged, about $18 per person, is one worthy of a high-tech roller coaster). The road surface is no longer the friction-free, slippery cobbles that had *carrinhos* careening down the hill. Toboggans now slide more slowly than they used to. And the lot of the *condutores* has changed, even if their outfits have not. They used to have to walk back up the hill, carrying or pushing the 68-kg (150-pound) sleds, but nowadays a taxi takes them up and a truck transports the toboggans.

and prized *azulejo* panels. The unimpeded views of Funchal are unbeatable.

Terreiro da Luta, at 876 m (2,873 ft), has its base about 1.5 km (1 mile) north of Monte, but climbs another 330 m (1,000 ft) to the top and offers yet another magnificent panorama of Funchal. It was here that the revered figure of Our Lady of Monte (now in the church below) was allegedly discovered in the 15th century.

On the summit is a monument to Nossa Senhora da Paz (Our Lady of Peace), dedicated to the end of World War I. Around the monument are anchor chains from French ships sunk in Funchal harbor by German torpedoes.

A bird's-eye view of Curral das Freiras, a splendidly isolated former nunnery.

Equally stunning views of Funchal and surroundings can be enjoyed at **Pico dos Barcelos**. Although at 355 m (1,164 ft) the altitude of the balcony is less than half that of Terreiro da Luta, the sweeping views from west to east and back into the terraced hillsides are superb. If you have brought your own transport, make a short detour to see the handsome landmark church of **São Martinho**. It's surprising to find such a large church in a relatively isolated farming parish.

Another 16 km (10 miles) north on the narrow, twisting road is **Curral das Freiras**, a village that until very recently was truly isolated from the outside world. The "Refuge of the Nuns" is a perfect crater surrounded by extinct volcanoes. The nuns in question fled here from Santa Clara Convent in the 16th century to escape raiding pirates. Protected on all sides — hidden is more accurate — by inaccessible mountains, and supported by rich volcanic soil and abundant sunshine, their settlement became permanent.

The village became famous for its cherries and chestnuts, and the popular liqueurs *ginja* and *licor de castanha*. The cakes here are also excellent. The village continued in splendid isolation until quite recently, when tunnels were finally bored through the mountains to bring the first roads. Fitting for a place once cut off from the secular world, villagers had to wait until 1986 before the first television pictures arrived.

Curral das Freiras is pleasant enough, but the quiet village is perhaps best experienced from above. The view peering down into the valley from the lookout point of **Eira do Serrado** (1,006 m/3,300 ft) is breathtaking. The whitewashed houses and red-tile roofs scatter about a sun-dappled, green terraced valley. If you opt for a coach tour, make sure a stop at Eira do Serrado is included (there's also great shopping and a newly built *estalagem*, or inn, here).

An alternative view is from the south, way across the valley, at the lookout point with the romantic name of **Boca dos Namorados** (Lovers' Nest). This is a difficult trek that, although feasible by car, is usually incorporated on the itinerary of jeep safaris. From here, the panorama sweeps round and takes in the entire valley (though even at 3,608 m/1,100 ft you'll still be close enough to hear the bell of the village church). The Alpine scenery looks as if it is straight out of Austria or Switzerland.

This man is a proud member of Camacha's wickerwork operation, which is both massive and well-known.

Camacha, back toward Funchal and east of the city, is a pretty village set at a refreshing altitude of nearly 700 m (2,300 ft). In the heart of willow country, Camacha is famous throughout the island as the heart of the wickerwork industry. Around 2,000 people in the region are employed crafting wicker furniture, hats, trays, decorative deer, and about anything you can imagine in wicker. Around Camacha and north of here you'll likely see the stripped willow soaked and left to dry, either by a river bank, propped up against a house, or in wigwam fashion in the fields. You may even see families sitting at the roadside, cooking the willow in cauldron-like vats and laboriously stripping off the bark.

Most of the weaving is done in the home, however, and the only place you are guaranteed to see craftsmen at work is in the slightly dingy basement of the **Café Relógio**. Despite its rather dull appearance and the crowds of people, this three-story "wicker-superstore" is an excellent place for shopping and refreshments — and just about the only highlight in town. The upstairs restaurant features Madeiran food and has excellent panoramic views.

Camacha is also the starting point for two excellent *levada* walks (see page 47), suitable for people of all ages and abilities. One heads west to Vale do Paraíso, the other northeast to Eira de Fora.

WESTERN MADEIRA

Western Madeira begins just beyond the capital's tourist zone. Ten km (6 miles) west of Funchal is **Câmara de Lobos** ("lair of the sea-wolves"). The peculiar name refers to the seals that once swam near the fishing village.

Colorfully painted fishing boats in the bay of Câmara de Lobos add spice to the seaside atmosphere.

Câmara de Lobos is more picturesque from afar than it is up close. It owes its reputation to its youthful, moreso than present, beauty. In 1950, Winston Churchill spent time on the island painting the fishing port, an interest that ensured its standing as an idyllic, old-world fishing village. The gaily-painted boats are still here, as is the protected, rocky natural harbor, but the old quarter overlooking the ocean has seen better days.

> As you enter from the direction of Funchal, the terrace where Winston Churchill sat and painted is just above the port. However, the best view of Câmara de Lobos is from the low-level *miradouro*, a few hundred yards back towards Funchal. If you want a good view of the village, drive to Pico da Torre.

The port area has resisted attempts at gentrification and fairly swaggers with macho atmosphere. Hard-drinking locals down *poncha* (sugar-cane brandy, lemon juice, and honey) in shadowy bars, while grizzled old fishermen play cards or repair their boats, awaiting their next trip. Close to the waterfront is a small, white chapel, an early 15th-century project that was later rebuilt (1723). The winery of **Henriques & Henriques** is also in town. Otherwise, there's not much for the tourist here, but you have to hand it to Câmara de Lobos for remaining a pure and simple working port.

Beyond Câmara de Lobos, the coastal road climbs for some 10 km (6 miles), passing through some of the richest agricultural country in southern Madeira, famous for the high quality of its grapes. Eventually it leads to the top of the mighty headland known as **Cabo Girão**. One of the highest sea cliffs in the world, it plummets 590 m (1,900 ft) to the Atlantic. The views east and west along the coast are sensational. Blue-and-white *agapanthus* cling to the top of the promontory, and pine and eucalyptus creep right to the edge, but an even greater degree of daring can be seen hundreds of feet below, where farmers have managed to salvage tiny plots of arable land, terracing them into little green postage stamps stuck onto the sides and base of the cliff.

The winding road continues on through the sprawling settlements of Quinta Grande and Campanário. The latter, an important grape-growing area, is also remarkable for its cliffside caves, used by local fisherman for storage purposes. A local boat trip is required to see them.

The next major settlement, heading westwards, is **Ribeira Brava** (if in a hurry, it can be reached in just 15 minutes on the *via rápida* highway from Funchal). The town's name, which means "wild river" or "ravine," seems hyperbolic for such an orderly and peaceful little community. Except in winter, Ribeira Brava's river is more of a tame trickle. The river heads due north, as does the road — straight across the island to São Vicente — making the ancient town of Ribeira Brava (established in 1440) an important junction. There are a couple of hotels here and a pleasant stony beach with umbrellas.

A couple blocks back from the beach, the main focus of attention is a tidy square, paved with black, egg-shaped stones from the beach, and its 16th-century church, with a blue-and-white tiled steeple. Next door is the small municipal market, while behind is the town center, featuring an attractive old church.

From Ribeira Brava, most coach excursions head north to São Vicente, as the road cuts through some of the best scenery on the whole island. However, those with more time can continue along the southwest coast.

Ponta do Sol is the next village after Ribeira Brava. As its name suggests, it is blessed with more than its fair share of sunshine. Only during the summer does it really come alive, however, when beach umbrellas are set out on the pebbly shore across from the small square. There are two buildings of note here: an 18th-century church and an Art-Deco cinema. As is frequently the case in Madeiran villages, the best views are from vantage points on the hillside road as it climbs up away from the village.

Past the tiny settlement of **Canhas**, notable for its statue of Santa Teresa and the Stations of the Cross, is a *miradouro* overlooking Madalena do Mar. About 10 km (6 miles) west of Ponta do Sol is **Calheta**, a banana plantation center and the only town of significance as

The village of Ribeira Brava is home to this distinctive tower in its town square.

you head west. Igreja Matriz, the parish church, dates to 1430 but was rebuilt in 1639: It features a handsome Moorish-style ceiling. Calheta is the site of recent tourism investment, but as of yet doesn't attract large crowds. From here, the best idea is to backtrack along the main road towards Funchal, either heading inland to Paúl da Serra or heading a bit farther east on your way toward Serra de Água and São Vicente.

Paúl da Serra ("High Moorland") comes as a surprise on this island with such luxuriant vegetation. A plateau that measures 17 km (11 miles) long by 6 km (3.6 miles) wide, the flat plain stands in dramatic contrast to the rugged mountains in the center of Madeira. The scenery and landscape of the plateau are reminiscent of the bleak moors of Scotland, and on clear days it is possible to see both the north and south coasts of the island. In good weather, hikers are drawn to its remote and barren character. If you are thinking of walking or hiking here, be warned that mists descend suddenly; you may want to go with a guide (see page 111).

On the road west to Porto Moniz, a minor road leads to **Rabaçal**, a beautiful valley popular among Madeirans at weekends and holidays. It is also the starting point for a couple of spectacular *levada* walks (see page 47). One is an easy, flat, and short (about 30 minutes roundtrip) trip to the **Risco waterfall**. The other takes about three hours and involves a pretty steep climb along the way to **25 Fontes** ("25 Springs") — as the name suggests, a verdant and water-filled spot. Both walks, indicated on almost all maps of Madeira (including the free one given out by the tourism office), are delightfully scenic.

At the island's extreme northwestern tip is **Porto Moniz**, located 70 km (44 miles), but seemingly a world away, from Funchal. A volcanic extension reaches out into the waves of the Atlantic, and the reefs form a series of protected natural pools. Small plots of land, divided by heath-tree fencing (to protect crops from the salt-laden wind) climb the hills

Flowers and volcanic rock commingle in Porto Moniz, at the edge of Madeira.

overlooking the sea. With few facilities other than a couple of hotels and restaurants on the coach-tour circuit, it isn't really a place to linger, unless the weather's warm and you want to go swimming or sit on the rocks and contemplate the ocean.

East from here, the coastal road is one of the island's star attractions. Often shrouded in mist, the two-lane road hugs the jagged coast and climbs the mountainside, clinging precariously to a narrow ledge. A rocky outcrop with a hole carved in it like an open window has lent itself to the name of the nearest settlement, **Ribeira da Janela** ("River Window"). Water gushes down from the mountains; some is diverted to hydro-electric stations, but a lot simply drains off into the sea, splashing off passing cars like a natural car wash or amusement-park ride.

This view of São Vicente gives us a portrait of one of Madeira's prettiest towns.

Seixal ("say-shall") is the only other settlement before São Vicente. The Sercial grape, used to produce the driest style of Madeira, is named for this pretty coastal village that is the center of a wine-growing district. Just beyond Seixal, heading east, it is well worth taking a short detour to make the steep climb up to the attractive spot of **Chão da Ribeira**.

São Vicente, perhaps the prettiest village on the island, begins at the point where the northern coastal road meets the north-south road heading 21 km (13 miles) to Ribeira Brava.

Levada trails, this one near Serra de Água, are a perfect way to take in the scenery.

The town lies just south of an unusual little chapel carved out of a rock. São Vicente's compact and well-cared-for center is pedestrian-only, and attractive shops and cafés look onto Igreja Matriz, a lovely church with a colorful painted ceiling depicting St. Vincent.

Tourism is making inroads, and restaurants have been designed with day-trippers in mind, but the village remains pristine. Larger restaurants and a hotel line the seafront, but the village itself is set inland, protected from the harsh ocean winds.

The newest tourist attraction in these parts is the **Grutas de São Vicente** (St. Vincent Caves), opened in 1997. Formed when a now extinct volcano erupted more than 400,000 years ago, the caves were carved by molten lava. The "tubes" formed are more than a kilometer (half mile) in length. In 1855 an Englishman discovered the caves, which, being a lava bed, do not have icy limestone stalagmites and stalactites but "lava drops" that look like thick whirls of chocolate mousse. In a low-rise building near the cave entrance is a small ethnographic museum, a place to see displays of local island customs and costumes as you wait a couple of minutes for the guided cave tour to begin.

High on a hill above the village is an odd church — actually a clockless clock tower — standing over a small chapel dedicated to Our Lady of Fátima. This isolated spot is a significant pilgrimage place, and can be seen for miles around.

From here, the road continues to cut its way through beautiful, verdant countryside until finally coming to a crest at the pass of **Boca da Encumeada** (626 m/1,007 ft). From this point you can see right to the north coast and well into the south, while stretching on each side are vast expanses of mountain scenery. This is one of the starting points for strenuous treks to Pico Ruivo (the island's highest peak, at 1,862 m/6,109 ft).

Of a more relaxed nature, one of the island's best *levada* walks skirts the edge of the mountain and takes in the entire

---

Levadas

Few things man-made on Madeira can rival its natural gifts. *Levadas* are the best of both worlds, simple irrigation channels that provide direct access to the best of the island's natural beauty. Cut no more than a few inches wide, and set a foot or two into the ground, levadas run more than 2,150 km (1,350 miles) around Madeira, and they've been here almost as long as the island has been settled.

The footpaths alongside each *levada* were built for maintenance purposes, but create a great network to explore the interior of the island. Some *levadas* are suitable for all ages; the only requirements are reasonable footwear and, at most, a taxi waiting at the other end. As *levadas* wind through the hillsides, most gradients remain gentle. Nonetheless, paths that follow the lie of the hillside can also give rise to unexpected vertiginous drops.

All you need to know about a handful of levada walks is contained on these pages, but for more detailed information and additional trails, see *Landscapes of Madeira* by John and Pat Underwood, sold in local bookstores.

valley, with views of the sea. Look for concrete steps opposite the Café Encumeada. The 45-minute walk along the water canal, more a stroll through a botanical garden than a hike, is lined with hydrangea and ferns and ends at a waterfall. A tunnel about halfway along provides chilly relief on a hot day.

> There is a much better chance of clear mountain-tops in summer months than during the rest of the year. If it's raining, know that it's only a 23-km (14-mile) drive from Funchal to Pico do Arieiro, and you can always try hiking again the next day.

Three km (1.5 miles) south of the pass, perched on the edge of Serra de Água, is a handsome and comfortable mountain chalet, the best of its kind on Madeira. The **Pousada dos Vinháticos** (*vinhático* is a type of Madeiran mahogany tree) enjoys the sort of views that many Alpine hotels would cherish. It's the perfect place for lunch or tea on the terrace, but many visitors, especially those with hiking on their minds, find it an ideal place to stay several days.

The valley on the opposite side of the road, south of the *pousada,* is known as **Serra de Água**, and lays claim to the distinction of being the island's first hydro-electric power station. In spite of the introduction of modern technology, however, the valley remains a quiet agricultural community tucked away in some of the island's lushest hills.

The road from here leads down into Ribeira Brava, where the *via rápida* motorway whisks you back to Funchal.

MADEIRA'S MOUNTAINOUS MIDDLE

The rugged mountain range that splits the island into north and south makes weather forecasting a difficult proposition on Madeira. One route to take in a good section of this picturesque terrain is to drive north (and up) from Funchal toward Santana on the north coast. There are beautiful vistas, secluded villages, and a range of exhilarating walks en route.

While it is usually warm and clear down in Funchal, the mountains are often shrouded in a wintry mist. This doesn't necessarily mean that you'll have no view once you start climbing, however. The tops of the mountains often jut through the clouds, a spectacular sight in itself. Madeira's microclimates are very difficult to judge, especially from below. If it looks clear, beat a hasty path up to Pico do Arieiro first thing in the morning. You should know by the time you arrive at Poiso whether or not the journey will be worth the effort.

At 1,818 m (5,900 ft), **Pico do Arieiro** is the second-high- est peak on Madeira, but the highest point reachable by car. As the road rises, the rugged countryside becomes spectacularly

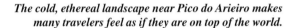

The cold, ethereal landscape near Pico do Arieiro makes many travelers feel as if they are on top of the world.

Island Flora

It's difficult to sing the praises of Madeira's abundant flora without resorting to cliché, but even hoary nicknames, such as "the Atlantic's Floating Flower Pot" and "God's Botanical Garden," aren't far from the truth. Few places on earth are so strewn with plant life, the majority of which is exotic (as opposed to native), originating from all parts of the world. Who can resist such a display of orchids, flamingo flowers (*anthurium*), and the vibrant, plume-like bird-of-paradise flowers (*strelitzias*)?

The spectacle of hibiscus (China), blazing bougainvillea (Brazil), and bird-of-paradise flowers (South Africa) lasts throughout the year. Others to look for include:

Spring: Jacaranda blossom above Funchal's Avenida Arriaga, lasting until June. Elsewhere on the island, see the painted trumpet (South America), the cockscomb coral tree, and the pastel-petal franciscea (both from Brazil), flame trees, and the unmistakable red-hot poker (South Africa), which fires up from May to August and contrasts with the cool white lily.

Summer–Autumn: The hills teem with flowers, and the common blue or white African lily provides cheery roadside color. Bright blue hydrangeas (China and Japan) are a familiar sight, while the delicate petals of the frangipani look hand-painted. In August, cassia flowers produce masses of yellow, lasting for

three months. The sunny golden trumpet and stiverbush, two South American varieties, bloom through this period as well. Even when in blossom, the dragon tree (found in the Canary Islands and Madeira alone) is a strange, primitive sight. During September, look for creeping podranea (South Africa) and in the hills, pink-and-white belladonna lilies.

Winter: In winter, the kaffir or lucky bean tree blooms with red flowers, and there are not only daisies, but daisy trees as well. Another curious tree to look out for is the kapok, also known as the silk-cotton tree. Its pink flowers blossom from September to November, and in spring a silky, cotton-wool-like fiber is produced, which is used for stuffing cushions and pillows. Poinsettia, a Christmas favorite, blooms in October and lasts until February or well beyond. The vine variously called golden shower or orange trumpet comes out in December and also lasts until February. Dramatic arum lilies are a common sight from November through to June.

Orchids are in their prime until May. Cymbidiums (Asia) are intensely grown for export, so too are cypripediums (various origins), which are known commonly as lady's-slipper.

The diversity of flora in Madeira is dazzling, from Protea flowers on the left, to the Flamingo flowers at right.

Trout circle endlessly at the hatchery in Ribeiro Frio, awaiting their final destiny.

barren, though plunging volcanic hillsides have been softened and greened by time. If you're driving, beware of sheep straying onto the road.

The lookout point at the windswept, lunar-like summit provides a 360-degree panorama. With its stratified canyon walls, a field of frozen lava, and boulders flung across the scene of volcanic catastrophe, it's a geologist's dream. During summer, the terrain is parched, while at other times of the year it's often covered with snow. The overnight temperature plunges below freezing most of the year, while the average annual temperature is less than 10°C (50°F). There is also six times as much rain here as in Funchal. If the arrival of clouds catches you unaware, a welcome place of refuge is a modern *pousada*, a good stop for lunch and popular overnight stay with hikers.

At 1,862 m (6,109 ft), **Pico Ruivo**, the rooftop of Madeira, is only 62 m (209 ft) higher than Pico do Arieiro, but much less accessible. The peak can be reached by an hour-long walk from Achada do Teixeira in the north, or the classic but strenuous, 4-hour roundtrip hike from Pico do Arieiro (see page 49).

The latter is well signposted, and there is a paved footpath, with drops protected by railings. The trek is popular; on a good day you will see several other walkers, so don't worry about losing your way. Warm clothing and hiking boots are essential, though, and in winter bear in mind that conditions on the mountains can be hazardous, with landslides removing parts of the path. Check weather conditions from the tourist information office in Funchal, then double-check at the *pousada* when you get there.

Back on the main road north (past Poiso) is the enchanting spot of **Ribeiro Frio**, more a bend in the road than a town. A microclimate in "Cold River" makes this an ideal stopover — the souvenir sellers along the main road are an indicator of the number of people that pop in. Victor's Bar, a restaurant resembling an Alpine chalet, receives most of them, warming visitors with log fires and freshly grilled trout from the trout hatchery across the road.

Adjacent to the restaurant is a tiny chapel and small botanical garden. The trout hatchery is a series of inter-connected concrete pools; the trout become increasingly bigger as you go along the pools. The botanical garden is not in the same league as the beautiful gardens you will see in Funchal, but it nevertheless claims to have examples of every species of flower, plant, and tree to be found on Madeira, and sprawls unpredictably along twisting paths among shady trees.

Ribeiro Frio is relaxing, but the real reason for its popularity are two **walks** that begin here. The shorter one, 2 km (1 mile) to the outstanding lookout point known as the **Balcões** ("balconies"), takes just 45 minutes roundtrip. After a stroll through the woods, you reach a platform that seems suspended in mid-air, with stupendous views across steep hillsides and dramatic ravines to the distinctive peaks of Ruivo and Arieiro. If it's not hidden in cloud cover, the sight certainly ranks as one of the most beautiful on the island.

The second walk is one of the island's most popular *levada* trails. It continues for just over 10 km (6 miles) until it reaches **Portela**, where a good restaurant offers sustenance to weary hikers. The walk takes most people about three hours, so you may wish to arrange for a taxi to collect you at Portela. An alternative short walk is to head out along the *levada* for a half hour or so (before steep drops begin), by which time you will certainly have been able to sample its charm, and then head back to Ribeiro Frio. Both options have food and drink waiting at the end.

The levada walk to Balcões ends here, with a sublime view across the valley.

The Road to Santana

North from Ribeiro Frio, toward the coast, is **Faial**, much photographed because of its picturesque setting at the foot of the Penha d'Águia. However, there's little of note in the village itself, aside from a handsome church and the Casa de Chá do Faial, which despite its name ("Faial Tearoom") is a standard restaurant with picture windows and fine roof-top panoramas.

The road winds westward to at least two memorable lookout points looking back at the village from the main road. **Santana** is home to a quaint but primitive style of housing — A-shaped structures known as *palheiros* (not to be confused with the A-shaped cow huts that dot the hillsides all over Madeira). The classic palheiro is a two-story white stucco with a brightly painted red door, red-and-blue window frames and shutters, and above all, a thatched roof.

Santana is frequently labeled one of the most attractive villages on the island, but its setting is the real star. The emerald hills and jagged coastline are reminiscent of Ireland's west coast. White houses shrouded in mist dot the slopes. The town itself is a rather straggly place with a modern town hall and no identifiable center. Two palheiros, perfectly painted in red, white, and blue, are the objects of many tourist cameras, while one immediately behind these remains a private home, its owners desperate to keep out gawkers.

Elsewhere, there are miniature palheiro dog kennels, and down by the river even the ducks have their own palheiro. There is also a furnished "showhouse" palheiro (not always open) next to the O Colmo restaurant, where you can see the extremely confined living space.

More thatched houses of a larger and more conventional kind are to be found 5 km (3 miles) south of Santana. **Queimadas** is a complex of cottage-style rest houses with attractive gardens. It's a lovely spot for a picnic, although if the weather is clear you might prefer to take the opportunity to ascend to the very top of the island. This is reached by a 10 km (6 mile) drive south of Santana, through the forest park of Pico das Pedras, up to **Achada do Teixeira** at 1,592 m (5,223 ft). From here, it's a two-hour walk roundtrip to Pico Ruivo (see page 47).

The scenery northwest of Santana is just as delightful. **São Jorge** has a fine, richly ornamented church, while past the

These palheiro *houses, a traditional form of island architecture, are found only in Santana.*

village there is a splendid panorama from the *miradouro* of **Cabanas**, over to the valley of Arco de São Jorge.

The road winds inland towards the picturesque, fertile countryside in the vicinity of **Fajã do Penedo** and on to the pretty village of **Boaventura**. To enjoy excellent views, follow the coast road down to the small peninsula of **Ponta Delgada**, where you can cool off by the rocks in the seawater swimming pool. From here it's just 5 km (3 miles) to São Vicente, at which point the road heads south to Ribeira Brava, then east back to Funchal.

EASTERN MADEIRA

The eastern section of Madeira isn't as mountainous as its center, but it has some wonderful coastal spots, a handful of attractive small towns, productive agricultural fields, and a long, surreal promontory that juts out into the Atlantic.

As you head out of Funchal, the village of **Santo da Serra** can also be reached via Camacha or from the Poiso crossroads. The altitude of 670 m (2,200 ft) produces refreshing breezes, and explains why several wealthy British expats have chosen to build *quintas* here and why so many affluent Madeirans still flee the hot Funchal summer up into these hills.

The most striking feature of Santo da Serra is its flatness; it may not be in the league of Paúl da Serra, but it is still large enough to accommodate a 27-hole golf course (see page 82). Even if you're not much of a golfer, you might still enjoy a stroll through the pleasant gardens of **Quinta da Junta**, once owned by the ubiquitous Blandy family but today public. A lookout point provides views across to Machico on the coast, and you can enjoy a drink at the golf club bar, set in what was once a *pousada*.

At **Portela** (662 m/2,172 ft), the views of the coast are striking. If you're lucky, you may see a hang glider take off from a nearby platform. **Penha d'Águia** dominates the northeast coast. This huge rock formation, towering at 590 m (1,935 ft), levels off to a flat top. The name, meaning Eagle Rock, is derived from its former inhabitants rather than its shape.

The village of **Porto da Cruz**, 6 km (4 miles) north, lies in the shadow of the rock. Here you will find one of Madeira's few sugarcane mills still working, pumping out steam as it processes the sugarcane to make *aguardente*, the local liquor. It doesn't operate all year round, however, and it is open to the public only in April. The village is neat and tidy, but there's nothing to detain you for very long.

Machico can claim to be Madeira's first settlement, the spot where João Gonçalves Zarco first came ashore on the island in 1419. Zarco ruled the western half of Madeira, while his fellow Portuguese captain and navigator, Tristão Vaz Teixeira, governed over the eastern half from Machico. A statue of Teixeira stands outside the town's 15th-century parish church, **Igreja Matriz**. King Manuel I donated the statue of the Virgin (over the altar) and the distinguished church portal. The latter is a fine example of the exuberant style of Manueline architecture.

From Machico's triangular "square," several streets lead to the seafront — a dark, pebbly beach with a small fort dated 1706. The local fishermen's quarters lie just east of the river, where cows graze along the banks, a scene unexpected in sub-tropical Madeira, where cows are usually confined to tiny huts.

At the northeast end of the island, one finds Porto da Cruz, nestled in among the steep mountainsides.

Machico is one of Madeira's boat-building centers, and on the beach you will probably see work in progress on both old and new vessels, the former being used for scrap. With the aid of EU funding, large, new tuna boats are being built to replace old stock. Follow the road all the way around the bay for a fine view across, east to west. The incongruous high-rise blot on the landscape directly opposite is the massive Hotel Dom Pedro, rather out-of-place in this low-key town, but an indicator of its tourism ambitions.

The churchtower of Igreja Matriz rises above Machico, Madeira's oldest town.

The road north heads inland after Machico. A huge, fenced-off area is under construction as a *zona franca* — tax-free business development area — intended to attract foreign investment. With so little in the way of industrial development elsewhere on the island, this zone is particularly startling.

The landscape of the eastern peninsula, known as the **Ponta de São Lourenço**, is more like Porto Santo and the Ilhas Desertas than Madeira. It is wild and windswept, and its limited vegetation a far cry from the lush green interior. Keen walkers enjoy this tip of the island, but for many it is a little too invigorating for comfort.

Caniçal was once a famous whaling port, but since whaling was banned in these waters in 1981, all that remains of this formerly lucrative industry is a Museum of Whaling and a few scrimshaw and whalebone souvenirs in a hut by the beach (more of the same is on sale at the car park at the end of the road heading east).

> Madeira is known for its microclimates. Even though it's a small island, the weather can change several times over the course of the day, or as you move just 5 km to a new spot. Clouds especially come and go with great alacrity, so don't despair if a day starts overcast. It may be clear as a bell in a matter of minutes, or in a spot just minutes away.

Although the **Museu da Baleia** (Whale Museum) shows a video of a whale hunt in 1978, the owner is the epitome of a poacher turned gamekeeper. Once commander of the Caniçal whaling station and thus responsible for taking 100–200 of the great creatures each year, he now devotes his energy to saving the whale and other marine life of the area. The 14-meter (45-foot) model of the sperm whale is a reminder of the leviathans that once swam in great schools in the waters off Madeira. Whales are still sighted here, but not frequently.

The beach of Caniçal now looks rather forlorn, with rotting hulks and flotsam and jetsam testifying to better days. Nevertheless, it's a working fishing port, complete with a selection of good fish restaurants. Close by, at **Prainha**, is the island's only natural sandy beach. Not surprisingly for a volcanic island, the sand here is black, and even this stretch is sometimes washed away.

The town of **Santa Cruz** is a pleasant place, with an attractive church dating from the 16th century. Across the main square, the town hall, in spite of having been modernized, retains a pair of splendid 15th- to 16th-century

*Framed by the cliffs and the ocean is Caniço de Baixa,
an attractive development of holiday homes.*

Manueline windows. A few streets away, the courthouse is
another survivor of that era, with fine verandas and an
impressive main staircase. Along the seafront is the modern
municipal market and a pebbly beach.

These days Santa Cruz is best known for the **Aeroporto
de Santa Cataria** (international airport) that serves Funchal
and all of Madeira. In 2000 it was still undergoing a massive
expansion. As you continue driving east, you actually travel
underneath the runway, which is supported on huge pillars
above you — a novel (not to mention rather sobering)
sensation both for those above and below.

The main road along the coast toward Funchal passes
Caniço, the first settlement of any real size. The original
village is built around an imposing 18th-century church,

while the new Caniço de Baixa is a sprawling proliferation of smart holiday homes visible from afar.

After roughly another mile, turn off the main road towards **Ponta do Garajau**, a holiday development popular with German visitors. The road ends at a fine *miradouro*, where a statue of Christ stands with arms outstretched (a miniature version of the statues at Rio de Janeiro and Lisbon). There is also a good view west to the Bay of Funchal; to the east, the modern resort on the small promontory is **Caniço de Baixa**, another favorite with German vacationers.

The road dropping down into Funchal winds past some of the town's smartest villas. The first landmark you'll see is the church of São Gonçalo in the parish of the same name. Also in the vicinity is the tiny, atmospheric chapel dedicated to Nossa Senhora das Neves (Our Lady of the Snows).

PORTO SANTO

The island of Porto Santo, 40 km (25 miles) northeast of Madeira, is the only other inhabited island in the archipelago, with a population of some 5,000. As desert islands go, it's not exactly undiscovered — it's accessible by ferry or very short flight — but only a handful of foreign visitors find these shores. Porto Santo is still, at heart, the resort of Madeirans, who seek what they have not: sand.

Porto Santo's prize is a long, golden beach, only recently touched by development. But that's not all that distinguishes Porto Santo from Madeira. In summer the smaller island is scorched and yellow, with rusty-colored rock and cliff formations. The island is mostly quiet, with a short, three-month summer season. Out of season, however, even the main town seems deserted.

The frequently rough sea crossing drops passengers at Porto de Abrigo, on the eastern tip of the island. (The return crossing, however, is never as bad.) From the dock it is a short taxi or bus ride, or a 20-minute walk, to **Vila Baleira** (sometimes referred to as **Porto Santo Town**), the island's only settlement of notable size.

The center of **Vila Baleira** is a small, triangular plaza, comprising a small town hall and a church now restored after more than three centuries of use. **Nossa Senhora da Piedade** (Our Lady of Piety) was originally founded just after the island's discovery during the early- to middle-15th century. The present church was rebuilt after pirates destroyed the original in 1667, though part of it, the Morgada chapel, did survive.

Porto Santo's claim to fame, beyond its sandy beach, is its link to Christopher Columbus. The town's major attraction is a house that stands next to the church, set back a little off the square: **Casa de Colombo** (closed weekends) dates from the

The recently restored Nossa Senhora da Piedade church in Vila Baleira has survived more than its share of pitfalls.

15th century and has recently been restored. It's an atmospheric little house, built from rough-hewn stone; it's not hard to imagine the great explorer living here.

The story of Columbus and the Madeiran archipelago is not entirely apocryphal, unlike so many other tales related to the islands. Columbus married Felipa Moniz Perestrelo, the daughter of the first Governor of Porto Santo, Bartolomeu Perestrelo. However, there is no strong evidence that he ever lived here. Still, the museum claims that around 1480 Columbus lived here for about two years and that young Diego Columbo was born a *Portosantense* in this house.

Regardless of the truth, Casa de Colombo is worth a visit. Displays include period pieces, memorabilia, replicas, maps, paintings, and sketches, though no personal effects or anything directly linked to the man himself. Another curious enigma about Columbus that has baffled historians is that no reliable likeness of him has ever survived. Take a look at the portraits in the museum, and then compare them with the dashing, modern bust of him in the public gardens by the quay.

The most interesting street in Vila Baleira is Rua João Gonçalves Zarco, on the other side of the river, running down to the sea. Here you will find the town's small market and a number of old shops and bars with plenty of character.

An Island Tour

Porto Santo is tiny (less than 11 km by 6 km/6 miles by 4 miles). It doesn't require much sightseeing, which is good, because most people just come to bake on the beach. Hiring a car is expensive, and what there is to see is usually near the main roads. Taxis will take you around the island, giving their own tours at fixed prices (see page 120). Pick up a leaflet from the tourist office and ask for a driver who can speak your language. Another alternative is to take a minibus tour with an agency such as Blandy's.

Heading around the island in a counter-clockwise direction, the first stop is the lookout point of **Portela** (163 m/535 ft). From here, you can survey the whole 9 km (6 miles) of the golden, sandy beach. Head north, however, and the desolate nature of the landscape is inescapable. Crop yield is poor, partly because of the chronic lack of water, and fields once tended are now deserted. Earning a living from tourism here is, to most, more appealing than toiling in the fields.

The island's highest peak, at 517 m (695 ft), is **Pico do Facho,** situated around 1.5 km (1 mile) due north of Portela. You'll need to don hiking boots to get to the summit. Its name, "Peak of the Torch," is taken from the warning beacons that were lit here in the days when French and Algerian pirates posed a threat to the island.

The circular road now arcs north to the diminutive village of **Camacha**, where the principal attraction is a picturesque old windmill — one of the last few still working on the island. If it is closed, ask locals if you can look inside; they're likely to fetch the friendly mill owner to come and open up for you. Nearby, a ramshackle winery with an antique wooden press produces the local Porto Santo wine. If it is closed, you can still sample the wine in either of the village's two restaurant-bars.

A minor road heads west out of Camacha to **Fonte da Areia** ("Sand Spring"), where the rugged coastline is particularly lovely. Sandstone cliffs and rocks have been weathered into interesting shapes and small caves. A spring filtering through the rocks is the source of the island's mineral water.

False Prophets, Magical Sands

The inhabitants of sister island Porto Santo are sometimes referred to by Madeirans as *profetas*, meaning prophets — the result of a strange episode in the 16th century, when a local shepherd started a religious cult. Not only did he say he could predict the future, he held people in sway by claiming the power to list their most intimate secrets and sins. Fortunately, the cult was short-lived and the *Portosantenses* resumed normality.

Magical powers of a different kind are also attributed to the island's beach, which is said to hold curative properties that alleviate all kinds of aches and pains. Many Madeirans and locals are convinced of its benefits.

This old windmill in Camacha still produces power,
which is a tribute to its ingenious design.

The main road continues its loop, bringing you just about back to Vila Baleira, before a minor road heads north again towards **Pico do Castelo**. It's only a couple of hundred yards from Pico do Facho, and from its height of 437 m (1,433 ft), accessible by car, provides a quite commanding view itself.

The old, rusted cannons are all that remain of the fortifications that once protected the islanders from pirates. Nowadays it's a popular spot for picnics and barbecues. Porto Santo's airfield (much larger than the one at Madeira before the latter was expanded), lies just below.

A favorite local picnic spot is **Morenos**, towards the southwest tip of the island, though close to, and looking out over, the north coast. It is neat and well-tended with sunshades, flowers, and seats, and enjoys a picturesque view over to the tiny **Ilheu de Ferro** ("Isle of Iron"). The last viewpoint of the tour is **Pico das Flores,** at 184 m (603 ft). From here you can see north along the beach; the only blot on the landscape is the unfinished Novo Mondo hotel — a notorious, 8-story white elephant completely out of proportion with the rest of the island.

Directly beneath Pico das Flores is the southern end of the beach and Porto Santo's easternmost point, known as **Ponta da Calheta**. The rest of the island's beach is a long, uninterrupted expanse, backed by attractive but slightly featureless dunes. Here, however, there are small bays with picturesque, rocky outcrops and you can enjoy a beautiful view across to the Ilheu de Baixo.

The beach at Ponte da Calheta sets itself apart from nearby beaches by its pretty views and rock formations.

SELECTED MADEIRA HIGHLIGHTS

Adegas de São Francisco. Old Blandy Wine Lodge, tasting rooms and wine museum.
Av. Arriaga, 28. Tel. 291/740 110. Guided visits Mon–Fri, 10:30am and 3:30pm, Sat 11am. Admission fee.

Sé. Funchal's 16th-century cathedral.
Largo da Sé (Av. Arriaga), Funchal. Open Mon–Sat, 7am–12:30pm and 4pm–6:30pm; guided visits, Mon–Sat at 9am and 11am, 4pm and 5:30pm. Free.

Museu de Arte Sacra. Religious Art Museum with important Flemish and Portuguese pieces from the 16th–18th centuries.
Rua do Bispo. 21. Tel. 291/228 900. Open Tues–Sat, 10am–12:30pm and 2:30–6pm; Sun 10am–3:30pm. Admission fee.

Quinta das Cruzes. Portuguese and foreign furniture and porcelain from the 16th to 19th centuries, in a mansion once lived in by Madeira's founder, Zarco.
Calçada do Pico, 1; Tel. 291/741 382. Open Tues–Sat, 10am–12:30pm and 2:30–5:30pm; Sun 10am–1pm. Admission fee.

Mercado dos Lavradores. Municipal market — flowers, fish, and vegetables.
Rua Dr. Fernao Ornelas, Funchal. Open Mon–Fri, 7am–4pm; Sat, 7am–1pm. Free.

Jardim Botânico/Parque do Loiro. Funchal's magnificent botanic garden and bird park.
Caminho do Meio (Quinta do Bom Sucesso), Funchal. Tel. 291/200 200. Open daily, 9am–5:30pm (museum, 9am–1:30pm). Admission fee.

Quinta do Palheiro Ferreiro. Spectacular private gardens on 30-acre estate, known for its camellias.
Palheiro Ferreiro (3 km. east of Funchal); Tel. 291/792 422. Open Mon–Fri 9am–1pm. Admission fee.

Jardim do Palácio do Monte. Handsome tropical gardens of 18th-century Quinta palace.
Caminho do Monte, 174; Monte. Tel. 291/782 339. Open Mon–Sat, 9am–6pm. Admission fee.

WHAT TO DO

SHOPPING

Madeira is an outstanding shopping destination, given its long and proud craft heritage. The island is renowned worldwide for exquisite handmade lace and embroidery, well-crafted wicker items, gorgeous flowers, and long-lasting Madeiran wines. Traditional, labor-intensive methods and quality are still respected in Madeira.

Unlike the Canary Islands, Madeira offers no tax concessions for visiting shoppers, so this is not the place to come in search of cheap electrical items, cameras, or watches.

Best Buys

Needlework. Madeira's hand embroidery is unsurpassed worldwide. This disappearing art form — still going strong in Madeira — is an amalgam of styles and techniques gathered over more than 150 years. Along with fortified wine, embroidery and lacemaking are Madeira's superlative exports, and in Funchal you have ample opportunity to visit factories or workshops where the final touches are put to these painstakingly produced items. However, you're unlikely to see much of their actual manufacture, as the vast majority of the work is done in the home by local women (some estimate that upwards of 10,000 are involved in the industry). Madeira creates and exports table linens, sheets, dresses, blouses, handkerchiefs, and even wedding dresses of extraordinary delicacy. Tapestries range from copies of Old Master paintings to traditional pastoral scenes.

If you're used to machine-made, mass-produced embroidered items, you may be in for sticker shock: a full set of meticulously detailed table linens can take up to two years to make, so prices aren't cheap (although, measured as a reflection of someone's salary for that length of time, they really are). If you value the time, effort, and craft that goes into these items, the price is likely to seem reasonable.

To be sure that any needlework item is the genuine article (as opposed to an inferior import or machine-made piece), look for a lead seal with an "M," the emblem of IBTAM — meaning it's been certified by the *Instituto de Bordado, Tapeçaras e Artesanato da Madeira* (Institute of Madeiran Embroidery, Tapestry, and Handicrafts), an official island organization that has a showroom/museum on Rua Visconde de Anadia, 44. There you'll find a tapestry known as the "Allegory of Madeira," which employed a total of 14 girls for three years and contains an estimated 7 million stitches.

> Madeirans do not take a siesta, but most businesses close for a one- to two-hour lunch break.

Wicker. Basket weaving and willow work, another of Madeira's most important export trades, also depend upon locals working out of their own homes. You'll find an outstanding array of wicker items — everything from picnic baskets and trays to tables, chairs, and decorative deer — throughout Madeira. While many items are attractive and inexpensive, the impracticality of taking them home — especially since wicker is not expensive in most parts of the world — might suggest opting for other souvenir items. Accustomed to exporting, though, most companies will send large items to Europe and North America for you.

Several factories allow tourist shoppers to see wickerwork in the making, an activity more interesting than it sounds: items are crafted not only with the hands and feet but occasionally the teeth as well.

Handicrafts. Though needlework and wicker are the biggest sellers, other craft items also make good souvenirs and gifts. **Boots** made from soft goat hide are part of the national costume (women's versions have red leather trim around the ankle). The boot and leather goods seller just outside the entrance of Funchal's Mercado dos Lavradores market is worth a visit. The boots worn by the *conductores* who push the Monte toboggans are available (as are the **straw hats,** old-style boaters, that they wear).

Ceramics and pottery are some of the most popular items throughout Portugal. Most of the items you'll find in Madeira, like pretty hand-painted plates, planters, jugs, and jars, come from the mainland — but if you're not traveling to other parts of the country, Madeira is still a good place to pick them up at bargain prices.

Other items include **marquetry,** a recently revived island craft that is featured on small boxes and pictures, and furniture. The **brinquinho** is Madeira's answer to the tambourine, in which miniature cymbals are clanged together by cos-

tumed dolls "dancing" round a maypole. You'll find thick **knitwear** — pullovers, hats, and gloves — at many shops in the mountains. Unexpectedly chilly weather might make these a good impulse buy. Many of these wintry items are imported from the north of Portugal.

Roadside pottery stands offer quality products and good prices as well.

Flowers. After a stay in Madeira, you're likely to wish your home could be one-tenth as verdant and full of flowers. Creating a lush Madeiran backyard won't be easy, but you can still take home souvenir flamingo flowers

> **How much does this cost?**
> *Quanto custa isto?*

(*anthuriums*), orchids, and bird-of-paradise flowers (*strelitzias*, or *estrelícias* in Portuguese). The latter in particular will last quite a while after your return home. Most shops will box these for storage in the airplane hold and deliver them either to your hotel or the airport on the day you leave. Taking delicate bouquets onto the plane may prove a bit more complicated.

Food & Drink. Madeira cake and wine are extremely long-lasting, so you can safely bring some back. Genuine Madeira cake, *bolo de mel* (or "honey cake"), sold in many different sizes, is a far cry from what you get at home. It's a delicious, dark, heavy cake, similar to gingerbread. Despite its name, it is made from molasses, not honey. It lasts for up to a year and goes very well with a dry Madeira wine. You'll also find traditional biscuits, honey, jams, and marmalades.

Most visitors take home a bottle or two of Madeira wine (see page 94). Connoisseurs with money to burn hunt down vintage bottles — you can still turn up rare bottles like a 1795 Barbeito Terrantez or 1900 Malavasia Solera (Henriques & Henriques).

Other alcoholic drinks that you might want to take home include *branquinha* (*aguardente* with a stick of sugarcane in the bottle), or a local liqueur such as *licor de maracujá* (passionfruit) or *ginja* (cherry liqueur).

Collecting. Madeira's colorful stamps, as well as coins, bank notes, and other items like postcards are of interest to many collectors. There's a shop specializing in all these items on Av. Arriaga, 75 (Marina Shopping, shop C; Tel. 291/223 070).

Where to Shop

Funchal's central area boasts the best variety of shops and local products on the island. The main shopping streets are Fernão Ornelas, Ferreiros, Queimada de Cima, and Queimada de Baixo, which form the downtown of Funchal. The majority of Funchal's shops are nostalgically small and personal.

For the best possible introduction to all of the island's handicrafts and saleable products, visit the **Casa do Turista** (Rua do Conselheiro & José Silvestre Ribeiro, 2; Tel. 291/224 907) on the seafront. The first few rooms are carefully laid out with pieces of antique shelving displaying fragile breakables; beyond them, you'll find a fairly conventional department store that stocks Portuguese ceramics, porcelain, wines, embroidery, dolls, and inexpensive souvenirs. Out back on the terrace is a "mini-village," where a little *palheiro* (see page 55), a house with a weaving loom, and an old-fashioned shop re-create a bit of old Madeira.

Competing with Casa do Turista is the new indoor handicraft and tourist market at **Eira do Serrado**. It sells excellent lace and embroidered items (most items are cheaper than they are

in Funchal), leather goods, and a great selection of vintage Madeiran wine, with bottles dating back to last century (for a hefty price, of course). Look for an inn, Estalagem Eira do Serrado, to be built next to the café here.

The market at Mercado dos Lavradores is always full to the gills with fish.

For needlework, visit any of Funchal's factories, which put the finishing touches on items and act principally as showrooms, selling direct to the public. The biggest and best-known is **Patrício & Gouveia Sucessores**, (Rua do Visconde de Anadia, 34; Tel. 291/222 723); it offers tours on weekdays. Keep an eye out for other outlets marked by small signs in doorways, including **Bordados Oliveira** (Rua Murças; Tel. 291/229 340) and **Madeira Supérbia** (Rua do Carmo, 27; Tel. 291/224 023).

While virtually every tourist shop displays wicker items, **Café Relógio** (Largo da Achada, Camacha; Tel. 291/922 114) wins for sheer volume. It is Madeira's "All Things Wicker," with items ranging from the most conventional to the most implausible. Alternatively, there are **Sousa & Gonçalves** (Rua do Castanheiro, 47) and **Unibasket** (Rua do Carmo, 42; Tel. 291/226 925), both in Funchal.

There are flower sellers set up along Av. Arriaga near the Sé (cathedral) and inside the **Mercado dos Lavradores**. A shop specializing in selling and packaging flowers for long-distance transportation is **Casa das Flores A Rosa** (Rua Imperatriz D. Amélia, 126; Tel. 291/228 800). The shop suggests that customers order flowers three days before departure.

For Madeira wines, the most atmospheric place to shop is the **Adegas de São Francisco** (see page 24), on Av. Arriaga next to the tourism office. It has nice tasting rooms (you can even taste vintage wines as old as 1920), a shop selling the three brands grouped under the Madeira Wine Company moniker (Blandy, Cossart Gordon, and Leacock), and a book and souvenir shop. Other possibilities in Funchal for wine include **Diogos Loja de Bebidas** (Av. Arriaga, 48) and **Garrafeira do Mercado Wine Shop** (in the Mercado dos Lavradores). The **Henriques & Henriques Vinhos** winery, producers of award-winning wines, and shop is located in Câmara de Lobos (Sitio de Belém; Tel. 291/941 551)

If you've run out of things to read by the pool, check out **Livraria Pátio** (Rua da Carreira, 43; Tel. 291/224 490), around the corner from the post office. It stocks books in English, French, and German (as well as Portuguese).

ENTERTAINMENT

Madeira can't rank with the Balearic or Canary Islands for nighttime entertainment; it's a much more low-key place. Although Funchal has its share of pubs, bars, discos, and even a well attended casino with revues, most visitors don't come to the island for evening entertainment.

The nucleus of the tourist nightlife scene consists mainly of the major hotels and their bars and nightclubs. At Funchal's **Casino da Madeira** (Avenida do Infante; Tel. 291/231 121), near the Pestana Carlton Park Resort & Casino, you can play blackjack, roulette, and take a turn at the slot machines. An admission fee is charged (good for a free drink and chips in the amount of admission); you will

Dance Roots

Many of Madeira's music and dance traditions date to the island's colonization. They evoke rural and courtship rituals, as well as less happy moments in the island's history. Dances reflect the importance of labor; jaunty jigs mimic the crushing of grapes with bare feet (a practice that has only recently died out) and slower numbers act out the carrying of heavy baskets.

The happy rhythm of these dances contrasts with the overtly somber *Dance of the Ponta do Sol*, which harks back to Ponta do Sol's days as a slave quarters. The steps are short; the feet, as if chained, hardly lifted off the ground; and the head is submissively bowed (slaves were forbidden to look their masters in the eye).

A group of musicians in traditional dress in Parque de Santa Catarina entertain those passing by.

need to take your passport if you wish to do more than hit the ground-level slot machines (the real gambling is upstairs). The casino is open until 3am Sun–Thur, and until 4am on Fri and Sat.

If gambling isn't your scene, the Casino entertainment complex goes for the *tropicalia* quotient with its **Copacabana Bar** (Tel. 291/233 111)**,** which has live music Wednesday–Saturday, and **Rio Restaurant,** which stages cabaret dinner shows and Brazilian samba extravaganzas (Tuesday–Saturday). Both are open until 4am.

The other principal hotel for nightlife is the Madeira Carlton (see page 128), which puts on similar theme evenings, plus classical concerts and children's shows. The Savoy (see page 128) also has a reputation for lively nightlife in its bar.

Young people head for **Teatro** (facing the City Park, next to the municipal theater; Tel. 291/759 959), **Dó Fá Sol** (Largo das Fontes; Tel. 291/241 464) and **Clube Avenida** on top of the Marina Shopping Center. Rua Imperatriz Dona Amélia (behind the Savoy hotel) has a number of restaurants and bars, including **Prince Albert**, an English pub, and **Salsa Latina** (Rua Imperatriz Dona Amélia, 101; Tel. 291/225 182), which has live music. Nearby, **O Fugitivo** (Rua Imperatriz Dona Amélia, 68) is a popular nightclub with nightly Brazilian dancers and transvestite shows (it's open until 6am). **Vespas Discoteca** (Av. Francisco Sá Carneiro, near the marina; Tel. 291/227 970) has a laser show and lots of sweaty youth; it's also open until 6am.

For more down-to-earth nightlife, several restaurants offer regular *fado* evenings. These include both **Arsénio** (Rua de

---

Madeiran Folklore & Colorful Garb

Madeiran street flower-sellers wear native costume — not only good for business, but required by law. Ladies in cheerful garb, as colorful as the flowers they hawk, gather alongside the cathedral at the main city market.

Younger girls wear the same red-and-yellow striped skirts, often with a red bolero jacket and red cape, for folk-dance demonstrations. Men wear white linen trousers and white shirts, and red cummerbunds. Black skullcaps, with curly tassels like candlewicks, are worn by both men and women, as are the native *botachãs* (literally, plain boots), made from tanned ox hide and goat skin. Women's boots are indicated by a red band.

Two musical instruments played are uniquely Madeiran: the *machête*, a guitar-like instrument plucked to a rather monotonous beat, and the extraordinary *brinquinho*, a percussion instrument that features tiny folk-dancing dolls holding bells and castanets.

Santa Maria, 169) and **Marcelinos** (Trav. Da Torre, 22) in Funchal's old town, and **O Pitéu** (Rua da Carreira). *Fado* songs, accompanied by classical guitar, generally deal with the hardships of seafaring life.

> **What time does it start?**
> *A que hora começa?*

Folk-dancing evenings are a regular feature at hotels; and one popular tour is a trip to Camacha's **Café Relógio** (see page 75), where the dancers are reputed to be Madeira's best.

Funchal's **Teatro Municipal** is the only place that regularly stages more theatrical entertainment. It is worth a visit, if only to see the theater itself. Dating from 1888, it has recently been restored to its original splendor, and produces most of the performing arts. It is the centerpiece of the annual music festival, here in June (see below).

The **Madeira Amateur Dramatic Society**, founded in 1993, puts on productions in English (and occasionally Portuguese), including "The Importance of Being Ernest," "A Christmas Carol," and "Last of the Red Hot Lovers." Inquire at the tourism office or check local publications (see page 116) for schedules.

FESTIVALS

Madeira celebrates four major festivals, among the best times to visit the island if you don't mind crowds.

Carnival. Staged in February (and occasionally March), Carnival is celebrated through the streets of Funchal with Brazilian-style samba rhythms — but don't expect the hedonism or sensuality of the type of celebrations in Rio or Tenerife, Spain. Funchal is much too restrained for that and, besides, its party is strictly small scale.

Flower Festival. This festival in late April or early May is a crowd pleaser. It includes floats — decorated in beautiful and inventive floral creations — parading through Funchal's

The children's parade at the flower festival is always a truly charming sight.

streets. Two events peripheral to the main parade should not be missed. One is the **children's parade**, in which each child carries a single flower and then places it in a hole in a "Wall of Hope" in the Praça do Município. Covered in flowers, the wall is a moving sight. Once the parade is finished, an **exhibition** of the award-winning flowers and displays is put on in a lovely old house in Rua dos Castanheiros.

Wine Festival. Festivals take place in several villages to celebrate the September harvest. You may even see *boracheiros*, men sampling the goods from traditional goat-skin bags once used to store and carry wine.

New Year's Eve. Madeira's biggest and most spectacular festival has earned a worldwide reputation. It jams Funchal's hotels every year; you will need to book accommodation many months in advance and pay a hefty premium. (Ironically, it's the one night of the year when you get the least sleep.) Many winter cruise ships anchor in Funchal harbor on December 31 to take part in the party. At 11pm, all the houses in town switch on all their lights, opening all the doors and windows, setting the hillside ablaze in light. The cruise ships crank up their flood lights, and the parties begin. As the New Year rings in, a splendid fireworks display erupts.

Several **religious festivals** also take place throughout the year, but one especially stands out. The **Feast of the Assumption**, known more parochially as the Festival of Nossa Senhora do Monte (Our Lady of Monte), is celebrated 14–15 August in Monte. Pilgrims flock from all around the island to kiss the image of the patron saint, and some ascend the final 68 steps to the church on their knees.

To many Madeirans who believe the Lady of Monte has carried them through troubled times, the pilgrimage is an obligation. The Monte church is akin to Lourdes for these Madeirans. The sick and crippled arrive in droves in search of miracle cures. Once the pious devotions are over, however, wine flows, fireworks explode, *espetada* (kebab) stalls flourish, and Monte regains normality for another 363 days.

SPORTS

With no beaches to speak of, and scarcely enough flat ground for a playing surface, Madeira may not be the first destination that springs to mind for a sporting holiday. However, there are sufficient opportunities for most active vacationers, and excellent ones for those who enjoy walking and hiking.

Spectator Sports. The only spectator sport on Madeira is **football** (soccer). Islanders are just as wild about *futebol* as mainlanders, and Funchal's premier team, in the first division of the Portuguese league, plays at the fine local stadium (on Rua Dr. Pita) during the season. See the local newspaper for schedule.

Walking & Hiking. Mountainous Madeira, with its unique network of *levada* trails (see page 47), is perfect for walkers of all ages and abilities. Such watercourses exist outside

Madeira, but nowhere are they so accessible and do they cover such great area. The island's irrigation system is composed of 2,150km (1,350 miles) of channels. The paths are mostly gentle but exhilarating just the same time.

More serious trekkers, with cross-country or mountain walking on their minds (and in their legs), can choose from a number of recommended hikes, including:

Boca da Corrida – Encumeada (moderate; 5 hours): views of Curral das Freiras and the valley of Ribeiro do Poco.

Pico do Arieiro – Pico Ruivo – Achada do Teixeira (moderate to difficult; 4 hours): a journey to Madeira's highest peak.

Ponta de São Lourenço (moderate; 4 hours): great rock formations, flora, and views of the Atlantic.

The Caniçal tunnel – Boca do Risca – Larano (easy; 3.5 hours): a walk along the north coast between Boca do Risco and Porto da Cruz; terrific flora and sea views.

All of these treks can be undertaken alone by experienced walkers or under the watchful eye of local guides. See "Guides and Tours" on page 111 for information on local outfitters that organize guided walks.

Golf. Golf in Madeira is a year-round sport; the island has 45 holes of championship golf divided between two courses, both esteemed for their scenic beauty. Every spring the Madeira Island Open, part of the P.G.A. European Tour, takes place at Santo da Serra Golf Club.

The 27-hole **Santo da Serra Campo de Golf** (Santo António da Serra; Tel: 291/552 321), which opened in 1991, is one of Europe's most exciting and spectacular golf courses, suitable for all levels. Designed by Robert Trent Jones, the course has stupendous views from the mountains to the sea below as its backdrop. The only drawback is the weather, for Santo da Serra has a wet micro-climate and fair-weather golf is relatively limited outside of summer. Green fees are 6,000 esc. for 9 holes, 10,000 esc. for 18 holes, and 14,000 esc. for 27 holes. For more information, contact <clubegolf@madinfo.pt>.

The newer **Palheiro Golf Club** (Tel. 291/792 116) is in the São Gonçalo hills 15 minutes east of the center of Funchal. The course, designed in 1993 by Cabel Robinson, has 18 holes and is set in the luxuriant Quinta do Palheiro Ferreiro gardens. So spectacular are the views over the

> If you're going to do some of the serious trails, take warm clothing, as the weather can change very abruptly. Hiking boots with good support and traction are a good idea to combat uneven or loose surfaces, and sunblock is necessary to fend off the strong Madeiran sun.

bay and the city that it is a great place to visit, let alone play golf. Expect to pay 11,700 esc. for green fees. Men's handicap maximum is 28; ladies' 36.

For information on golfing in Madeira and links to both golf clubs, visit the web site <www. madeira-golf.com>. Green fees at other courses average 5,000 esc. for 9 holes and 9,000 esc. for 18 holes.

Tennis. Flat land is at such a premium in Funchal that even the likes of Reid's and Hotel Savoy can only afford two tennis courts each. If your hotel does not have its own court, try **Quinta Magnolia Park** (Tel. 291/764 598), where the facilities are excellent (including floodlights) and inexpensive. The park also has squash courts and an exercise trail.

Horseback Riding. Lessons and cross-country riding are offered by the Associação Hípica da Madeira (Quinta Vale Pires, Caminho dos Pretos, São Gonçalo; Tel. 291/792 582), just outside Funchal. Horses can also be rented from the Riding Club of Choupana at Hotel Estrelícia (Tel. 291/792 5 82) and the Quinta do Pântano (Casais

Boats in a Funchal marina bide their time, waiting to conquer the high seas.

Próximos, Santo da Serra; Tel. 291/552 577).

Horseback riding runs between 1,500–3,000 esc. per hour.

Swimming. Although much of Madeira's coast drops dizzily into the sea, offering little or no safe access for bathers, there are a number of pebbly bays and beaches. Sadly, Madeira's one and only (black) sandy beach, at Prainha, is isolated and not very attractive. Better bets are **Ponta do Sol** and **Ribeira Brava** where, during summer, beach umbrellas are put up and locals and tourists crowd onto the rocky shores. You can also have a dip in the semi-natural pools at **Porto Moniz** on the extreme northwest tip of the island.

True beach lovers should hop islands to the 9 km (6 miles) of sands of **Porto Santo** (though sunshine is only really guaranteed there from June to August). You can either fly on TAP/Air Portugal (15-minute flight) or take the ferry (which leaves daily at 8am; Tel. 291/226 511).

Most of Madeira's good hotels have their own swimming pools, but if yours doesn't, year-round swimming is open to the public at the excellent **Complexo Balnear do Lido** (Lido Swimming Complex; Tel. 291/762 217) in Funchal's Tourist Zone. Here you will find two main pools, plus a children's pool, sunbathing along the terraces and rocks by the sea, and surprisingly good catering facilities. What's more, it's cheap. The only drawback is, of course, the large crowds in summer. Another good, inexpensive public pool is in **Quinta Magnolia Park.** Some of the larger hotels, such as the Savoy, allow non-residents into their pool areas, but at a price guaranteed to exclude locals. **Ponta Delgada** has a public pool by the sea.

Diving. Sub-aquatic enthusiasts are in luck in Madeira: along the Garajau coastline one of Europe's first underwater nature reserves was created. Besides abundant, multi-colored fish, there are also shipwrecks to explore. Sea temperatures vary between 18° and 24° C (64–75° F).

The clear blue waters around Madeira have attracted the attention of four diving schools. Tubarão Madeira (Tel. 291/794 124; e-mail <tubarao.madeira@gmx.de>), located in the hotel Atlantic Palms on Praia Formosa, 3 km (2 miles) beyond Funchal, offers wreck-, night-, cave-, and NITROX-diving. Scorpio Divers, based at the old Lido (Complexo Balnear do Lido, Funchal; Tel. (mobile) 96/686 18 46), is the only British Sub-Aqua Club school; it offers everything from beginners' courses and single dives to advanced tuition. An alternative school is the Atalaia Diving Club in Caniço (Hotel Roca Mar; Caixa Postal 23, Caniço; Tel. 291/934 330; fax 291/933 011), which offers diving equipment for hire and various courses.

Expect a single dive to cost around 5,000–7,000 esc., while a novice diving course (including equipment hire) will run 50,000 esc. or more.

Big Game Fishing and Boat Trips. In the deep Atlantic, just beyond Madeira's shallow waters, you can catch — according to the season — giant blue marlin, bonito, tuna (big-eye, blue-fin, and yellow-fin), barracuda, swordfish, wahoo, and shark (hammerhead, maco, and blue). The best deep-sea fishing is from June to September. **Turipesca** (Tel. 291/231 063) charters set out from Funchal Marina. **Captain Peter Bristow** also runs big game fishing expeditions. Contact him at Quinta das Malvas, Rua da Levada da Santa Luzia 124 (Tel. 291/220 334; e-mail <p.bristow@mail.EUnet.pt>).

Big-game fishing expeditions cost upwards of 25,000 esc. per person per day; non-fishing spectators may pay as little as 5,000 esc. to go along for the ride.

CHILDREN'S MADEIRA

While there are no purpose-built attractions aimed at children, and no real beaches on Madeira, most kids should find the island an enjoyable experience, especially if your visit coincides with any of the major festivals (see page 79 and Calendar of Events, below). A number of sightseeing attractions should also appeal to children, as should Madeira's outdoor activities and scenic beauty. And when all else fails, the pools (at most hotels; see "Swimming," page 84) are enough to satisfy almost any child.

Among attractions, both the **Jardim Botânico** (Botanic Garden), with its bird park, and the gardens at **Quinta do Palheiro Ferreiro** are good targets for kids. The park on the hill of **Monte** makes a good playground, while the ride down in a wicker toboggan is straight out of an Old World theme park (though surely tame for older kids). The cost to ride the toboggans at Carros do Monte is 1,800 esc. per person.

Activities for slightly older children include **horseback riding** and *levada* **walks**. A very enjoyable nature day — identifying plants and flowers, dipping toes into the refreshing irrigation canals, cooling off in tunnels, having a picnic on a hillside — can be had at any of the levada paths highlighted in this book. The festivals with greatest appeal for the kids are the famous **Flower Festival,** with its childrens' parade and "Wall of Hope," and **Carnaval**.

CALENDAR OF EVENTS

February/March	**Carnaval** (Grand Carnaval Show and Public Carnaval Procession)
Last week April/ first week May	**Flower Festival** (and Ceremony of the First Wall of Hope)
June	**Madeira Music Festival** (Funchal's Teatro Municipal and Cathedral)
23–24 June	**São João da Ribeira** Funchal (St. John's Feast)
28–30 June	**São Pedro** Ribeira Brava (St. Peter's Feast)
9 September	**Nosso Senhor dos Milagres** Machico (Our Father of Miracles Feast)
July	**Folk Dancing Festival** (Santana)
First weekend August	**Madeira Wine Motor Rally**
Early September	**Madeira Wine Festival** (Grape harvesting in Estreito de Câmara de Lobos, with shows and exhibitions)
December	**End-of-year festivities** (Christmas lights and exhibitions on consecutive weekends leading to a big celebration and firework display on 31 December)
6 January	**Festa dos Reis** (Three Kings Festival and close of festivities)

EATING OUT

Funchal has been catering to visitors since Victorian times. While it's not the dining capital of Portugal, there are plenty of good restaurants that will satisfy almost any guest. For international or *haute* cuisine, the best places are in the hotel zone, the up-market far end of the Old Town, and touristy marina establishments. If you would rather go native and eat with locals, try the side streets around the cathedral, Rua Carreira, or the cheaper part of Old Town.

Meal Times

Traditional opening times are adhered to by most Madeiran restaurants, with lunch (*almoço*) served from around noon to 3pm and dinner (*jantar*) from around 7 to 10pm. Some restaurants in Funchal offer all-day service, not closing after lunch, and you will never have any problems finding cafés serving snacks, if not full meals.

> **Salt and pepper are seldom placed on the table. You will be given them if you ask, though:** *Sal e pimenta, faz favor.*

When it comes to breakfast (*pequeno almoço*), Madeirans start their day with only a bread roll and a cup of coffee. Hotels, however, usually serve the standard international buffet, with bacon and eggs as well as cold meats, cheese, fruit and cereals.

What to Eat

Madeira has typical dishes of its own in addition to Portuguese specialties. As a rule, the food is simple, uses fresh ingredients, and is served up in hearty portions.

A Madeiran trademark is the excellent island bread, *bolo do caco,* which is unleavened and nearly always served with

The interior of this tavern in Funchal is everything a bar should be: cozy, friendly and inviting.

garlic butter (*com manteiga de alho*). Special *bolo do caco* stalls are set up at festivals.

Starters. Soup is always on the menu. The best is usually Madeira's own *tomate e cebola*, a delicious soup made from tomatoes and onions, and very often served *com ovo* (with a poached egg floating on top). A Portuguese staple, *caldo verde* (literally, green soup), is a thick broth of potato purée with finely-shredded cabbage or kale. Another soup from the mainland is *açorda*, thicker yet and made with bread and garlic.

Basic fish restaurants serve *caramujos* (winkles), which look disgusting as you winkle them out from their tiny shells, but taste fine, and *lapas grelhadas* (grilled limpets). The latter are a meatier version of mussels (some of them taste almost like liver) and are served grilled in the shell. At

A baker in Funchal shows off his latest batch of Bolo do Caco — unleavened bread — at the flower festival.

the other end of the price spectrum, look out for smoked swordfish (*espadarte fumado*), a Portuguese delicacy which is a little like smoked salmon, but tastes less sweet and has a coarser texture.

Fish and Seafood. Madeira's specialty, seen on menus across the island, is the *espada*, a fearsome-looking, ink-black, eel-like beast, which can grow to around 1 m (3 ft) in length and has long, needle-sharp teeth. Despite its appearance, the nasty creature has delicious, flaky white meat. Some restaurants will boil them, but more often they are fried, often with a banana, which complements the flavor surprisingly well. Note that espada and espadarte (swordfish; see above), though similar sounding, are quite different animals.

The other island fish is tuna (*atum*), a solid, meaty-textured fish served in steaks (*bife de atum*) and often with a Madeira wine sauce (*a Madeirense*). Maize or cornmeal (*milho*) deep-fried in cubes (also an island speciality) is often served with tuna, and is offered as a standard accompaniment to many meals in *típicos* around the island.

You will also find a wide selection of other fish on the menu, usually grilled or fried, including: *pargo* and *besugo*, which are types of sea-bream; *garoupa* and *cherne*, types of

> A menu that quotes a price — usually for shell-fish or fresh fish — as *"preço V."* means variable, or market, price. Clarify the day's market price before ordering.

grouper; and *bacalhau*, the famous, Portuguese salt-cod, served in many ways. It is often served in a casserole, which tends to hide its distinctive, preserved flavor. Try it *cozido* (boiled). Other fish are shark, swordfish, and *bodião* (parrot-fish).

Two slow-simmering Portuguese favorites that appear on fish restaurant menus are *caldeirada* and *cataplana*. The former is a rich stew made from fish, potato, tomato, and onion, whereas the *cataplana* is actually the hinged pressure cooker, into which goes a mixture of clams, ham, sausage, onion, garlic, parsley, white wine, and paprika. (Ingredients may vary according to what type of *cataplana* is on the menu.)

Two local favorites are octopus (*polvo*), served cold as a salad, hot, fried, or stewed; and squid (*lulas*), grilled, fried, or stuffed (*recheado*). Shellfish do not flourish in Madeiran waters, and all prawns and lobsters are imported.

Meat. *Espetada* (which is not to be confused with *espada* or *espadarte*; see page 90) is the typical Madeiran meat dish, a kebab of beef traditionally threaded on a laurel stick. In most restaurants, however, it will be on a metal skewer with a hook on one end, which is hung vertically from a special stand, so everyone in the restaurant can see what you are eating. It's

A variety of fresh fruits is attractively displayed at the Marcados dos Lavradores.

grilled over burning laurel, and is usually tasty, but it can also be rather tough. For something easier on the jaw, try pork in wine and garlic (*porco de vinho e alho*), which is marinated, tenderized, and then grilled.

Chicken (*frango*) is always on the menu — whether it's served plain, grilled, African-style (as in *piri-piri*, when it's basted in a sauce of hot chili peppers, then grilled; very hot), or in a Goan-inspired curry sauce.

Ox tongue (*lingua*) served with Madeira wine sauce is another Portuguese specialty. **Desserts.** Portugal's *pudim* or *flã*, a type of crème caramel, is always available, as is ice cream (*gelado*). A good restaurant will usually offer seasonal fruit after your meal, but you may have to ask for it. The island has an excellent range of exotic fruits, so sample them fresh from the market if not in a restaurant. A favorite is *anonas* or custard apple (from Peru). Split in half, the flesh is soft and white, with large black pits. To some its taste is like its name, a sort of custard-like apple, while others liken it (rather more fancifully) to strawberries and cream. A specialty of several tourist restaurants is fruit *flambé*.

Table Wines

There is just one brand of Madeiran table wine, *Atlantis Rosé*, and it is sold throughout the island. Most good restaurants stock a full complement of Portuguese wines (top restaurants will also offer foreign labels), many of which are excellent.

Portuguese wines, while not as well known as those from Spain and France, across the board are quite good, and several regions produce truly excellent

> Nearly every restaurant in Madeira serves a *couvert* — an assortment of appetizers, including bread and butter, that appear to be free but are usually not. You will be charged anywhere from 100 to 800 esc. for the items. If you do not touch them, however, in theory you should not be charged for them.

wines. You need do nothing more than tell the waiter *tinto* (red) or *branco* (white), and you can't go wrong. However, several of the best wine-producing regions have names whose use is controlled by law (*região demarcada*), and it's worth seeking out wines from the best regions. Dão and Douro in the north of Portugal produce vigorous reds and flavorful whites. Wines from the Alentejo region are also highly regarded.

Vinho Verde (literally "green wine"), popular in the north of Portugal, is named for its youth, rather than its color, and it has a slight fizz. It goes well with simple fish and seafood dishes.

The two most celebrated Portuguese wines, port and Madeira, are primarily known as dessert wines, but they may also be sipped as aperitifs. The before-dinner varieties are dry or extra dry white port and the dry Madeiras. These should be served slightly chilled. After dinner, sip one of the famous ruby or tawny ports (aged tawnys are especially good) or a Madeira dessert wine.

Madeiran wine, which is held in high esteem throughout the world, is first-class both in taste and presentation.

Madeira Wine

The history of the island's eponymous drink, famous the world over, is as full and well-rounded as a bottle of the best vintage *Malvasia*.

When the island was first settled during the 15th century, Prince Henry ordered Zarco to plant vines, brought to the island from Crete. Although wine was not planned as an important export trade, it became one of the most important products of the island, thanks to a combination of its notable quality and Madeira's position on the shipping lanes to the East and West Indies. The island was an obvious stopping point where water, fresh food, and, of course, wine, could be taken on board. With the rise of the British colonies in North America and the West Indies, Madeira wine was soon established as a favorite on both sides of the Atlantic, and shipped all over the British Empire.

When Charles II of England — who was married to Catherine of Bragança, a Portuguese — decreed in 1665 that all goods shipped to the Americas had to sail from England, Madeira was exempt, giving the island a practical monopoly on the wine trade.

Initially, Madeira was not a fortified wine, but gradually the addition of grape brandy became common practice in order to stabilize it on long sea voyages. During the 18th century, it was discovered that shipping the wine actually improved its longevity as well as its flavor. Producers realized that tropical heat was the key ingredient, and towards the end of the century, pipes of Madeira were loaded as ballast on transatlantic journeys in order to cook them as much as possible.

Madeira Wine — Lore and Legend

It was William Shakespeare who first gave Madeira wine a literary platform, when in *Henry IV* Falstaff is accused of selling his soul for a leg of chicken and a goblet of Madeira. (It seems of trifling importance that Henry IV actually died before the discovery of the island, let alone the wine!) In 1478, the Duke of Clarence went one better than Falstaff. Accorded the noble's privilege of electing his own means of execution, he chose to be drowned in a barrel of *Malmsey*.

Sir Winston Churchill once ordered a bottle of 1792 vintage in Reid's Hotel, then further delighted his guests by placing a napkin over his arm and assuming the duties of waiter. Madeira wine didn't win favor with just the British, however. It was used to toast the American Declaration of Independence, and drunk at the Inauguration of George Washington, who was said to consume a pint of Madeira at dinner daily. Benjamin Franklin and Thomas Jefferson were also Madeira connoisseurs.

When it became impractical to send barrels on round trips, conditions for heating the wine had to be reproduced at home. The easiest way was simply to store barrels in lofts that soaked up abundant sunlight. Subsequently, special lodges called *estufas*, centrally heated by hot water pipes, were employed; this system is still in use today, subjecting each cask to a temperature of 35°C (95°F) for six months.

It remains a mystery how Madeira survives a process that would ruin any other wine. Moreover, the heating process renders the wine virtually indestructible. A bottle of Madeira can be kept for many months uncorked without suffering any deterioration, even when other types of fortified wine (such as port) would deteriorate quickly under such conditions. For this reason, there are Madeira wines from the early 1800s that are entirely drinkable today.

Choosing a Bottle. There are four types of Madeira, each named after the grape that gives that style of wine its distinctive flavor and characteristics. The lightest and driest is *Sercial*, which has a full-bodied, nutty flavor, not unlike an *amontillado* sherry. It is best served chilled as an aperitif. *Verdelho*, which is classified as medium-dry, should be served slightly chilled. A tangy aperitif, it's also recommended as an accompaniment to soup. *Bual*, likely introduced by the Jesuits in the 17th century, is a rich and port-like Madeira with a

Food preparations

If you want to make very sure you get that steak or fresh fish prepared the way you want it, here are key words to know when ordering:

Roasted	**assado**	Grilled	**grelhado**
Boiled	**cozido**	Fried	**frito**
Well done	**bem passado**	Medium	**mal passado**
Rare	**ná conta**		

It's never difficult to find a bite to eat here, as there is a large variety of seaside restaurants to choose from.

splendid honeyed taste and an underlying acidity, which means that it can cut through sweet desserts and is also a good accompaniment to cheese. Finally and most famously, *Malvasia* (also known as *Malmsey*) is the richest of all, and is usually served following a meal. It was the first grape introduced on the island, brought by early settlers from Crete.

All the Madeira wines, with the exception of vintage, are made from blends of several years, the youngest component of the blend being the stated age of the wine on the label; *Finest* is a blend in which the youngest is at least three years old, and *Reserve* and *Special Reserve* wines are at least five and 10 years old, respectively. The very best, however, are *Vintage* wines, produced with the crop of a single type of grape from a single year, and only bottled after aging in oak casks for a minimum of 20 years. The longer the wine stays in the cask, the better it will be. The wine is then kept for another two years before sale.

If you really want to impress the folks back home, buy a bottle of *1862 Vintage Bual* or *Sercial* for a mere 90,000 escudos or so ($450). If your budget doesn't stretch to that, you can pick up more recent vintages for around 7,000 escudos.

Other Island Drinks

After Madeira, the most famous island drink is *aguardente*, a powerful sugarcane distillation, which varies in taste from virtually unpalatable firewater to smooth, aged brandy. Look for the term *velha* (old) on the label unless you have an iron constitution. Add lemon juice and honey to *aguardente* and you have *poncha*, a delicious drink that belies its ferocious base.

Other liqueurs are distilled from the island's fruit, two notable examples being a cherry brandy from Curral das Freiras (see page 37) called *ginja*, and *licor de maracujá*, passion-fruit liqueur (don't confuse it with the soft drink, *refrigerante de maracujá*). The local lager, *Coral*, is also an excellent beverage. If you don't drink alcohol, you may enjoy the bottled mineral water produced in Porto Santo, but this can be an acquired taste.

To Help You Order...

| Could we have a table? | **Queríamos uma mesa** |
| I'd like a/an/some... | **Queria...** |

bread	**pão**	pepper	**pimenta**
butter	**manteiga**	potatoes	**batatas**
coffee	**um café**	rice	**arroz**
dessert	**sobremesa**	salad	**salada**
fish	**peixe**	salt	**sal**
fruit	**fruta**	sandwich	**sanduiche**
ice cream	**gelado**	soup	**sopa**
meat	**carne**	sugar	**açucar**

| menu | **ementa** | tea | **chá** |
| milk | **leite** | wine | **vinho** |

...and Read the Menu

alho	garlic	**amêijoas**	baby clams
ananás	pineapple	**arroz**	rice
atum	tuna	**azeitonas**	olives
bacalhau	cod (salted)	**besugo**	sea-bream
bife (vaca)	steak (beef)	**bolo**	cake
borrego	lamb	**cabrito**	kid
camarões	shrimp	**caranguejo**	crab
cavala	mackerel	**cebola**	onion
chouriço	spicy sausage	**churrasco**	grilled meat
coelho	rabbit	**cogumelos**	mushrooms
costeletas	chops	**cozido**	boiled
dobrada	tripe	**enguias**	eel
ervilhas	peas	**estufado**	stewed/braised
feijões	beans	**figos**	figs
framboesas	raspberries	**frango**	chicken
gambas	prawns	**gelado**	ice cream
guisado	stew	**laranja**	orange
legumes	vegetables	**leitão**	suckling pig
linguado	sole	**lombo**	fillet
lulas	squid	**maçã**	apple
mariscos	shellfish	**melancia**	watermelon
mexilhões	mussels	**molho**	sauce
morangos	strawberries	**ovo**	egg
peixe	fish	**perú**	turkey
pêssego	peach	**porco**	pork
presunto	ham	**queijo**	cheese
robalo	seabass	**salmonete**	red mullet
salsichão	large sausage	**sobremesa**	dessert
uvas	grapes	**vitela**	veal

HANDY TRAVEL TIPS

An A–Z Summary of Practical Information

A

ACCOMMODATIONS (See also RECOMMENDED HOTELS starting on page 127 and CAMPING on page 104)

Hotels and hotel-apartments (*aparthotels*) in Madeira are graded by the government from 2 stars to 5 stars. Below the rating of hotel is *estalagem*, which loosely translates as "inn." These may be simple hotels away from the main tourist areas, or they may be extremely comfortable, personal inns. The categories below estalagem are *albergaria*, *residência*, *pousada* and *pensão* are usually small bed-and-breakfast hotels with basic facilities. However, a handful of estalagens, albergarias and pousadas are the equivalent of four-star hotels.

Madeira is unique in also offering *quinta* accommodation. *Quintas* are gracious mansions and villas, usually set in splendid gardens, brimming with antiques, and restored to offer a standard of accommodation (and prices) equivalent to a 4- or 5-star hotel. They do not offer all the sports or facilities and amenities of a top hotel, but in terms of character and personal service they are often much better. All are limited in number of rooms, so book early. Early booking is also recommended if you want to stay on the island between Christmas and New Year's Eve (see page 80).

Pousadas offer the chance to experience local hospitality and cuisine. There are two *pousadas* on Madeira (neither of which is government-owned, as pousadas are elsewhere in Portugal): the Pousada dos Vinháticos on the north-south road from Ribeira Brava to São Vicente, and the Pousada do Pico do Arieiro, on top of the mountain of the same name. In keeping with the general *pousada* principal, these both enjoy tranquil, scenic settings away from the main tourist areas.

I'd like a single/double room.	**Queria um quarto simples/duplo.**
with bath/shower	**com banho/chuveiro**
What's the rate per night?	**Qual é o preço por noite?**

Madeira

AIRPORT *(aeroporto)*

Madeira's **Santa Catarina** international airport (Tel. 291/524 941 or 291/524 362) is located in Santa Cruz, 22 km (14 miles) east of Funchal. It used to have one of the shortest passenger runways in Europe until it was enlarged in 2000. The entire airport is still undergoing a massive expansion, with plans to begin attracting direct flights from North America for the first time.

From the airport to Funchal takes about 35 minutes by taxi or an hour by bus. (During rush hour, allow double the time.) Several rental car agencies have service desks at the airport, while elsewhere in the terminal is a small tourist information kiosk, currency-exchange office, restaurant and bar.

From Santa Catarina airport, visitors can either take the city bus (400 esc.), with multiple stops, or a taxi, which has posted set fares (between 3,200 and 4,800 esc.) to Funchal's tourist or hotel zone, or downtown.

The new airport on the island of **Porto Santo** (Tel. 291/982 146) is used as a local stop by a subsidiary of TAP Air Portugal, and there are some direct flights to and from Lisbon and Oporto.

Where can I get a taxi?	**Onde posso encontrar um táxi?**
How much is it to downtown Funchal?	**Quanto custa para ir ao centro de Funchal?**
Does this bus go to Funchal?	**Vai para Funchal este autocarro?**

B

BICYCLE RENTAL *(aluguel de bicicleta)*

You can rent a mountain bike, motor scooter, or motorcycle from **Joyride** (Tel. 291/234 906), in the Comercial Olimpo shopping mall near the Casino Park hotel in Funchal.

BUDGETING FOR YOUR TRIP

With a favorable exchange rate, Madeira may well be cheaper than many other European island destinations.

Transportation to Madeira. Many Europeans fly direct to Madeira aboard regularly scheduled and charter flights. Flights from England and Germany are likely to cost anywhere from $600 to $900 roundtrip or more. For those traveling from beyond Europe, the flight will be a considerably greater expenditure and portion of your overall budget — probably at least $1000 from North America. Economical package deals — airline and hotel — are usually available. Until direct flights are initiated, flights from North America (and many European cities) go through Lisbon.

Accommodations. Hotels at the top levels are comparable to large European cities. However, many at the two-, three-, and four-star rating are comparatively good values. A double room with bath per night in a 3-star hotel averages 9,000–15,000 esc.; 4-star hotel, 12,000–24,000 esc.; 5-star hotel, 25,000–40,000 esc.; *pousadas* 13,000–18,000 esc.

Meals. Even top-rated restaurants may be surprisingly affordable compared to most European capitals. Portuguese wines are quite good and very attractively priced, even in fine restaurants. A 3-course meal with wine in a reasonable establishment averages about 2,500–5,000 esc. per person. Many hotels offer half- and full-board plans.

Local transportation. Buses and taxis are reasonable. A bus to the center of Funchal from the hotel or tourist zone is less than 300 esc.; a taxi costs between 700-1,000 esc. (add a fare supplement of 20% on weekends, public holidays, and between 10pm and 7am).

Incidentals. Your major expenses will be excursions, entertainment, and daytime sporting activities. Renting a car is a good idea to allow maximum flexibility, but be sure to budget for the cost of a rental as well as gas, which is costly, as in most of Europe. Economy car rental will run between 5,000 and 8,000 esc. per day (including collision insurance and taxes); gas per liter is unleaded 185 esc., diesel 125 esc.

Nightclub and disco covers are high, as are drinks once inside. Casino (admission only) is 800 esc.; casino plus show and dinner 8,000 esc. Gamblers would be wise to budget for the possibility of losses. A folklore or fado show, including dinner, runs about 5,000–8,000 esc.

Madeira coach trips from Funchal cost about 5,000 esc. for a half-day, 8,000 esc. for a full day. Island-hopping to Porto Santo by air is about 15,000 esc. roundtrip; by ferry, 10,000 esc. roundtrip.

C

CAMPING *(campismo)*

There are two official camping sites on the Madeira archipelago, one in Porto Moniz and the other in Porto Santo, in the town of Vila Baleira. The campground in Porto Santo is the most visited campsite in Madeira. For more details contact: **Parque de Campismo do Porto Santo** (Vila Baleira, 9400 Porto Santo, Madeira; Tel. 291/982 160). You could also contact the **Madeira Camping Service** (Estrada Monumental/Hotel Baía Azul; Tel. 291/ 776 726; fax: 291/762 003 e-mail <info@madeira-camping.com>) or visit their web site, <www. madeira-camping.com>.

Is there a campsite near here?	**Há algum parque de campismo por aqui perto?**
May we camp here?	**Podemos acampar aqui?**

CAR RENTAL/HIRE *(carros de aluguer)* (See also DRIVING on page 107 and BUDGETING FOR YOUR TRIP on page 102)

There are both local and major international car rental agencies in Funchal (most near the hotel and tourist zones) and at the airport. Prices vary significantly, so shop around.

You must be at least 21 and have held a valid national (or international) driving license for at least one year. You will need to present a recognized credit card when booking. Third-party fire and theft insurance is included in the basic charge, but many firms quote col lision damage waiver (CDW) as an extra (usually between 1,000 and 1,500 esc. per day). Without this, you could be liable for any damage or loss to your vehicle, however caused, so you are strongly advised to accept it. Check with your credit card company before departure to verify what it covers when used to pay for the rental (many will cover the collision damage waiver and theft of vehicle protection). A government tax of 12% is added to the total rental bill when booking locally.

A weekly economy rental (such as a Nissan Micra) starts at around 35,000 esc. per week. In addition to many local companies, you'll find: **AVIS** (Largo António Nobre, 164; Tel. 291/764 546); **BUDGET** (Estrada Monumental, 239; Tel. 291/766 518); **EUROP-CAR** (Estrada Monumental, 306; Tel. 291/765 116); and **HERTZ** (Estrada Monumental, 284; Tel. 291/764 410).

I'd like to rent a car.	**Queria alugar um carro.**
tomorrow	**para amanhã**
for one day/week	**por um dia/uma semana**
Please include full insurance.	**Que inclua um seguro contra todos os riscos, por favor.**

CLIMATE (*clima*)

Madeira is generally warm and spring-like all year, making it an excellent winter retreat for northern Europeans. However, winter months can be relatively wet and the winds noticeably stronger. The rainiest period is from October to December, with an average of 6 to 7 days of rain per month, but you can still usually count on an average of 6 hours of sunshine a day. From May to September, the air is warm and somewhat humid. The typical pattern, year-round, is a clear, bright morning, with clouds rolling down from the mountains in the afternoon. For warm, clear weather, ideal for mountain walking, summer is your best bet.

Average daily charts follow:

Madeira

	J	F	M	A	M	J	J	A	S	O	N	D
min°C	13	13	13	14	16	17	19	19	19	18	16	14
°F	56	56	56	58	60	63	66	67	67	65	61	58
max°C	19	18	19	19	21	22	24	24	24	23	22	19
°F	66	65	66	67	69	72	75	76	76	74	71	67

Sea temperature

°C	17	17	17	17	18	19	20	21	22	23	20	18
°F	63	63	63	63	64	66	68	70	72	73	68	64

CLOTHING (*roupa*)

Warm-weather clothes will be fine in summer, but even then pack a pullover for mountain excursions. Winters are mild with the occasional shower, so a light, rainproof jacket may come in handy. Also in winter, you will definitely need wool (and waterproof) clothes for inland trips. If you're planning on walking you will need sensible footwear, but unless you are intent on tackling some of the more arduous trails, you won't need hiking boots.

Though an island getaway, Madeira has long been a place where visitors dress up for tea and formal dinners. Although there's less formality these days — shorts and T-shirts are fine during the day — Reid's formal restaurants still require men to wear a dark suit and tie; many wear black-tie to the winter restaurant. At other luxury hotel and restaurants in Funchal, jacket and tie are generally expected. Nightspots such as the casino are now more relaxed, and a jacket and tie are no longer the rule.

Will I need a tie?	**É preciso gravata?**
Is it all right if I wear this?	**Vou bem assim?**

CRIME AND SAFETY (*delito*) (See also EMERGENCIES on page 110 and Police on page 119)

Although Madeira is one of the safest places in the world for tourists, factors such as poverty (which does exist here, especially in small villages) inevitably make temptation irresistible for some. Follow the same general rules that you would elsewhere. Never leave anything of value in your car, even if it is out of sight. Burglaries of holiday apartments are rare, but leave any valuables in a safe-deposit box, or with the hotel reception. You must report any losses to the local police within 24 hours and obtain a copy of your statement for insurance purposes.

I want to report a theft.   **Quero participar um roubo.**

CUSTOMS AND ENTRY REQUIREMENTS *(alfândega/visto)*

Americans, Canadians, and many other nationalities need only a valid passport — no visa — to visit Portugal. EU nationals may enter with an identity card. The length of stay authorized for most tourists is 90 days (60 for US and Canadian citizens).

Currency restrictions. Visitors from abroad can bring (or exit with) any amount of local or foreign currency into Portugal, but sums exceeding the equivalent of 2,500,000 esc. in foreign currency must be declared on arrival.

Customs. Free exchange of non-duty-free goods for personal use is permitted between Portugal and other EU countries. However, duty-free items still are subject to restrictions; check with authorities before you go.

I've nothing to declare.   **Não tenho nada a declarar.**

It's for my personal use.   **É para uso pessoal.**

D

DRIVING

There are many good reasons not to drive on Madeira: car rental and gasoline are expensive, taxis are relatively cheap, and the tortuous mountain roads can be hard on one's nerves. But if there are many cons, then some of the pros may be equally compelling. You may well enjoy the challenge of the winding roads, and, of course, you have maximum flexibility with your own set of wheels.

Madeira

Road conditions. It is only worth considering driving into Funchal if you are staying well outside town (at Machico or Garajau, for instance). If you do, expect traffic jams. The roads across the island are mainly two-lane and well-paved, but, especially in the mountains and along the north coast, can be murderously twisting. These demand confident, relaxed drivers.

Rules and regulations. The rules are the same as on the Continent: drive on the right, overtake on the left, yield right of way to all vehicles coming from your right. Speed limits are nominally 90 km/h (56 mph) outside built-up areas and 60 km/h (37 mph) in built-up areas. Average cross-country speeds are well below 60 km/h. Seatbelts must be worn and children under 12 are not allowed in the front seats. Motorcycle helmets should also be worn at all times.

Fuel costs. At press time, gas per liter was: unleaded 185 esc., diesel 125 esc. Prices, controlled by the government, should be the same — or very close to it — everywhere you go. Many gas stations are 24-hour, and all accept credit cards.

Parking. Funchal is served by reasonably priced car parks at either end of town. Parking in the center is virtually impossible, except the "blue zone" (metered parking) along Av. do Mar e das Comunidades Madeirenses (facing the marina). You will have few difficulties elsewhere on the island.

If you need help. If you belong to a motoring organization affiliated with the **Automóvel Clube de Portugal** (ACP), you can make use of their services free of charge. The Funchal office is at Rua Dr António José Almeida 17-2°; Tel. 291/ 223 659. You will have no problem finding well-equipped garages in Funchal, but elsewhere you may have to rely on the services of the local mechanic.

Road signs. Aside from the standard international pictographs, you may encounter the following:

Alto	Halt
Cruzamento	Crossroads
Curva perigosa	Dangerous bend/curve
Descida íngreme	Steep hill
Desvio	Detour
Encruzilhada	Crossing
Estacionamento permitido/ proibido	Parking permitted/ No parking
Guiar com cuidado	Drive with care
Máquinas em manobras	Men working
Obras	Men working
Paragem (de autocarro)	Bus stop
Pare	Stop
Pedestres, peões	Pedestrians
Perigo	Danger
Proibida a entrada	No entry
Seguir pela direita/esquerda	Keep right/left
Sem saída	No through road
Trabalhos	Men working

Are we on the right road for...?	**É esta estrada para...?**
Fill the tank, please with...	**Encha o depósito de...**
three star/four star	**normal/super**
My car's broken down.	**O meu carro está avariado.**
There's been an accident.	**Houve um acidente.**

E

ELECTRICITY *(corrente eléctrica)*
The standard current is 220-volt, 50 cycle AC. For US appliances, 220v transformers and plug adaptors are needed.

Madeira

| I need an adaptor/a battery, please. | **Preciso de um adaptador/ uma pilha, por favor.** |

EMBASSIES/CONSULATES/HIGH COMMISSIONS *(embaixada; consulado)*

Several countries maintain consulates in Funchal. For serious matters, people are usually referred to their embassy in Lisbon.

American Consular Agency: Avenida Luís de Camões, Ed. Infante, Block B, 4th floor; Tel. 291/743 429

British Consular Agency (also for Commonwealth citizens): Avenida Zarco, 2; Tel. 291/221 221.

Lisbon Embassies

Australia (use UK Embassy): Rua de São Bernardo 33; Tel. 21/392 40 00.

Canada (Embassy/Consulate): Avenida da Liberdade 144, 3°; Tel. 21/347 48 92.

Republic of Ireland (Embassy/Consulate): Rua da Imprensa à Estrela 1, 4°; Tel. 21/396 15 69.

South Africa (Embassy): Avenida Luís Bivar 10/10 A; Tel. 21/353 50 41.

UK (Embassy): Rua de São Bernardo 33; Tel. 21/392 44 00.

US (Embassy/Consulate): Avenida das Forças Armadas 16; Tel. 21/727 33 00.

Most embassies and consulates are open Monday–Friday, from 9 or 10am until 5 or 6pm, with a lunch break lasting 1–2 hours.

| Where's the British/American embassy? | **Onde é a embaixada inglesa/ americana?** |

EMERGENCIES *(urgência)* (See also HEALTH AND MEDICAL CARE on page 112)

The emergency number for police, fire or ambulance is **112**.

The new Funchal hospital has a 24-hour emergency ward; call Tel. 291/705 674. Outside Funchal, ask for the local *Centro de Saúde* (Health Center).

G

GAY & LESBIAN TRAVELERS
A web site, <www.portugalgay.pt>, contains a travel guide for gays and lesbians, with information in English and other languages. It has little specific information relating to Madeira, but has a message board for postings.

GETTING TO MADEIRA (See also AIRPORT on page 102)
Air Travel. There are regular inexpensive charter flights to Madeira from Great Britain (Manchester, New Castle, Glasgow) and most major cities in Western Europe. British Air flies directly to Madeira from London Gatwick. The national Portuguese airline is TAP/Air Portugal (Tel. 888/328 26 71 anywhere in Portugal; Lisbon, 21/841 69 90; New York, 212/969-5775; London, 171/828-0262). It flies from several European cities to Funchal via Lisbon or Porto.

The flight time from London to Madeira is around 3 hours 30 minutes, and from Lisbon to Madeira 1 hour 30 minutes. It is no longer possible to sail to Madeira by cargo ship. Big cruise liners stop off at the island, but often only long enough for a brief sightseeing tour.

GUIDES AND TOURS (See PUBLIC TRANSPORTATION on page 120)
One of the preferred ways of seeing Madeira is by coach. Several operators basically all go to the same places, but charge different rates for different services. Standard itineraries include: West of the Island; East of the Island, including Pico do Arieiro; a half-day covering Monte/Curral das Freiras/Picos dos Barcelos; guided *levada* walks; and jeep safaris to out-of-the-way places such as Boca dos Namorados (see page 38) or Paúl da Serra. Not all of these are good value; the *levada* walks and the Monte trip are simple and inexpensive to do by yourself.

Other tour-operator itineraries cover a day-trip to Porto Santo, including an island tour (this is only recommended in summer, when sunshine and calm sailing are the norm), but you can also make your own way to the island and take a half-day minibus tour. Half-day boat trips cruise up and down the Madeiran coast, while other outings from Funchal Marina include a trip to the Ilhas Desertas, or a full day's sailing, including lunch, free wine, and the opportunity for swimming.

Information on tour operators, including Blandy's and other agencies, is available from the Funchal tourism information office and most hotels. Highly recommended **Lido Tours** (Shopping Center Monumental Lido; Tel. 291/762 429, fax 291/762 171; e-mail <info@lido-tours.com>) offers small-size (van) island tours, both full- and half-day; *levada* walks; and mountain walks. **Turivema** (Turismo Verde e Ecológico da Madeira) focuses exclusively on guided outdoors ecological tourism; contact them at Edifício Baía, Shop Nº 1, Estrada Monumental, 187; Tel 291/763 898; fax: +351 291 766210; e-mail <info@madeira-levada-walks.com>. **AMP Travel** (Tel 291/762 666; fax 291 762 171; e-mail: <info@madeira-portugal.com>) offers traditional coach island tours, guided walks, and even helicopter rides.

We'd like an English-speaking guide/an English interpreter.	**Queremos um guia que fale inglês/um intérprete de inglês.**

H

HEALTH AND MEDICAL CARE (*saúde*) (See also EMERGENCIES on page 110)
Standards of hygiene are generally high; the most likely illness to befall travelers will be due to an excess of sun or alcohol. Madeiran tap water (*água*) is safe to drink and tastes pretty good. Bottled mineral water — *agua com gas* (carbonated) or *sem gas* (still) — is sold everywhere; the Porto Santo brand has a strong taste not to everyone's liking.

Mosquitoes are present in summer, so an anti-mosquito device that simply plugs into your wall and emits a vapor that is noxious to the insect, but not to you, is worthwhile (available at airport shops).

There are 67 health centers situated around the Madeira island, and one at Porto Santo. *Farmácias* (chemists/drugstores) are open from Monday to Friday from 9am–1pm and from 3pm–7pm, Saturdays from 9am–1pm. On the door of every pharmacy you will find postings of after-hours pharmacies.

Tourist offices carry lists of doctors and dentists who speak English.

For more serious illness or injury, **Hospital Cruz de Carvalho** (Av. Luis de Camoes; Tel. 291/705 600) is the island's largest hospital and has English-speaking staff. Reach the local **Red Cross** (Cruz Vermelha) at Tel. 291/741 115.

Medical insurance to cover illness or accident while abroad is a good investment. EU nationals with EU form E111 obtained well before departure can receive free emergency treatment at Social Security and Municipal hospitals in Madeira. Privately billed hospital visits are expensive. If you don't take the form with you, it's a matter of paying on the spot and making claims on your travel insurance later.

Where's the nearest (all night) pharmacy?	**Onde fica a farmácia (de serviço) mais próxima?**
I need a doctor/dentist.	**Preciso de um médico/dentista.**
an ambulance	**uma ambulância**
hospital	**hospital**
an upset stomach	**dôr de estômago**
sunburn/a fever	**queimadura de sol/febre**

HOLIDAYS (*feriado*)

The following is a list of national holidays in Portugal.

1 January	**Ano Novo**	New Year's Day
25 April	**Dia da Liberdade**	Freedom Day

Madeira

1 May	**Dia do Trabalho**	Labor Day
10 June	**Dia de Portugal**	National Day
15 August	**Assunção**	Assumption
5 October	**Dia da República**	Republic Day
1 November	**Todos os Santos**	All Saints' Day
1 December	**Restuaração/Dia da Independência**	Day of Restoration/ Independence
8 December	**Imaculada Conceição**	Immaculate Conception
25 December	**Natal**	Christmas Day

Movable dates:

Carnaval	Shrove Tuesday/Carnival
Sexta-feira Santa	Good Friday
Corpo de Cristo	Corpus Christi

Madeira also celebrates 1 July (Discovery of the Island), 21 August (municipal holiday), and 26 December (Boxing Day).

Are you open (closed) tomorrow?	**Estão abertos (encerrados) amanhã?**

LANGUAGE

Portuguese, a derivative of Latin, is spoken in such far-flung spots as Brazil, Angola, Mozambique and Macau — former colonies of Portugal. Your high-school Spanish may help with signs and menus, but is unlikely to unlock the mysteries of spoken Portuguese. The Portuguese spoken in Madeira and the rest of Portugal is more closed and guttural-sounding, as well as faster, than that spoken in Brazil.

The *Berlitz Portuguese Phrasebook and Dictionary* covers most situations you're likely to encounter during a visit to Portugal. Also useful is the *Berlitz Portuguese-English/English-Portuguese Pocket Dictionary*, containing a special menu-reader supplement.

Here are some useful phrases to get you going (see also the front cover flap of this guide):

Good day/afternoon/evening	**Bom dia/Boa tarde/Boa noite**
Goodbye	**Adeus**
please	**faz favor (por favor)**
thank you (masculine/feminine speaker)	**obrigado/obrigada**
yesterday/today/tomorrow	**ontem/hoje/amanhã**
day/week/month/year	**dia/semana/mês/ano**
where/when/how	**onde/quando/como**
how long/how far?	**quanto tempo/a que distância?**
left/right	**esquerdo/direito**
cheap/expensive	**barato/caro**
hot/cold	**quente/frio**
old/new	**velho/novo**
open/closed	**aberto/fechado**
vacant/occupied	**livre/ocupado**
early/late	**cedo/tarde**
What does this mean?	**Que quer dizer isto?**
Please write it down.	**Escreva-mo, por favor.**
Have you something less expensive?	**Tem mais barato?**
Help me, please.	**Ajude-me, por favor.**
Get a doctor, quickly.	**Chame um médico, depressa.**
How do you do/Pleased to meet you.	**Muito prazer.**
How are you?	**Como está?**
Very well, thank you.	**Muito bem, obrigado/obrigada (masc/fem speaker).**

Madeira

Days

Sunday	**domingo**
Monday	**segunda-feira**
Tuesday	**terça-feira**
Wednesday	**quarta-feira**
Thursday	**quinta-feira**
Friday	**sexta-feira**
Saturday	**sábado**
What day is it today?	**Que dia é hoje?**

M

MAPS

Madeira is a small island with relatively few roads, so orientation is easy. The tourist information offices in Funchal and Porto Santo will supply you with a free map that includes both the island and capital and has several of the most popular *levada* trails drawn on it. For almost all purposes, even driving across the whole of the island, the free map should be sufficient. However, more detailed maps are published by the Instituto Geográfico e Cadastral, obtainable at local bookshops. The best map available in Britain is the Bartholomew Holiday Map. Serious walkers should buy a copy of *Landscapes of Madeira* by John and Pat Underwood (Sunflower Books), which includes specially drawn walking tour maps and details many *levada* trails.

MEDIA *(jornal; revista; radio; televisão)*

Europe's principal papers, including most British dailies, are on the newsstands the day after publication. *The International Herald Tribune* and in some places *USA Today* appear on the day of publication. Popular foreign magazines are sold at many kiosks. The only local English-language publication is the free monthly, *The Madeira Island Bulletin* (also available in German, *Madeira Aktuell*). You can pick up a copy at the tourist office in Funchal. If you can understand a little Portuguese, the daily *Jornal da Madeira* newspaper gives you a weather forecast and museum and temporary exhibition details, among other things.

Madeira has its own TV channel and also picks up mainland Portuguese programs. Most large hotels and some bars also have satellite TV for screening football matches and other sporting events. For details of what's on, pick up a copy of the *Jornal da Madeira*. Tune into Tourist Radio (96 FM) for news and features of tourist interest on the island, broadcast in several languages (English, 5:45–6:30pm Monday–Friday). The BBC World Service and Voice of America can be heard on shortwave.

Have you any English-language newspapers/magazines?	**Tem jornais/ revistas em inglês?**

MONEY (*dinheiro*) (See also BUDGETING FOR YOUR TRIP, on page 102)
Currency (*moeda*). The national currency is the escudo (abbreviated esc. or PTE). Price tags at first look worrisome, since they usually involve many digits around a $ sign — which replaces the decimal point (5,000$00 esc. is equal to 5,000 escudos). The escudo is divided into 100 centavos, although you aren't likely to see centavo coins these days. Coins now in use are 1, 5, 10, 20, 50, 100 and 200 esc. Banknotes come in denominations of 500, 1,000 (known as one *conto*), 5,000 and 10,000 esc.

The Euro, the common European Union currency, was adopted in January 1999. Although prices appear in both escudos and Euros, the euro remains an electronic banking currency until January 2002, when Euro notes and coins will begin to circulate. After a transition period of six months, the escudo will be removed entirely from the market.

Currency Exchange (*banco; câmbio*). Normal banking hours are Mon–Fri 8.30am–3pm. Some banks remain open later and at weekends to change money. There is also a 24-hour exchange office at the airport. Beware that changing money can be outrageously expensive — banks either levy up to 12% in commission or charge a flat fee of around £10/US\$20, regardless of amount changed, so ask first. Automatic money-exchanging machines (ATMs) provide by far the best exchange rates.

At press time, US \$1 = 210 escudos; £1 = 317 esc.

Credit Cards (*cartão de crédito*). Standard international credit cards are widely accepted. In some shops and restaurants, especially in small villages, however, you may not be able to use a credit card.

ATMs (*caixa automática*). Automatic teller machines outside banks, identified by the MB (MultiBanco) sign, are widely available. You can get cash (Portuguese escudos; maximum of 40,000 esc. per day) with a Visa or Mastercard, or other debit card on one of the international networks like Cirrus or Plus, provided you know the personal identification number (PIN). The PIN number should be four digits.

Traveler's Checks. Less necessary now that ATMs have proliferated across the world, international traveler's checks (such as Thomas Cooke or American Express) can be cashed at any bank, though a high flat-rate fee is charged for changing traveler's checks. Paying by check is invariably more expensive than by cash, due to the lower rate of exchange. You will need to show your passport.

Can I pay with this credit card?	**Posso pagar com cartão de crédito?**
I want to change some pounds/dollars.	**Queria trocar libras/dólares.**
Can you cash a traveler's check?	**Pode pagar um cheque de viagem?**
Where's the nearest bank/ currency exchange office?	**Onde fica o banco mais próximo/ a casa de câmbio mais próxima?**
How much is that?	**Quanto custa isto?**

OPEN HOURS (*horas de abertura*)
Though Madeirans do not take a siesta, most businesses close for a one-to two-hour lunch break. Shops and offices are generally open 9am–1pm and 3–7pm weekdays, and 9am–1pm Saturday. Most museums open between 10am and 5pm weekdays; several close 12:30–2pm, and most are closed on Monday and public holidays. Banks are open 8:30am–3pm Monday–Friday; currency exchange offices 9am–1pm and 2–5pm Monday–Saturday (closed Saturday afternoon).

Café-restaurants may be open all day, whereas more up-market establishments close after lunch and reopen for dinner.

Are you open/closed?	**Está aberto/fechado?**

POLICE (*polícia*)(See also EMERGENCIES on page 110)
The national police, identified by their blue uniforms, are generally helpful and friendly and often speak a little English. If you need help or have an emergency, dial Tel. 112. The main police station in Funchal, where there is a lost property section, is Rua João de Deus, 7 (Tel. 291/222 022).

Where's the nearest police station?	**Onde fica o posto de polícia mais próximo?**
I've lost my... wallet/bag/passport	**Perdi... a minha carteira/o meu saco/o meu passaporte**

POST OFFICES (*correios*) (See also TELEPHONE on page 122)
Post offices are indicated by the letters CTT (*Correios, Telégrafos e Telefones*). Mailboxes are of British pillar-box design and are painted bright red. The main post office in Funchal is on Avenida Zarco between Av. Arriaga and Rua Carreira. It's open 8:30am–8pm Monday–Friday (9:30am–1pm Saturday). Local branches have

shorter opening hours. You can buy stamps from tobacconists and kiosks, as well as at post offices.

A letter or postcard up to 20 g to EU countries costs 100 esc.; to the rest of the world, 140 esc. Mail may take up to a week to reach a European destination. There is also a 3-day "Azul" (express) service.

Where's the nearest post office?	**Onde fica a estação de correios mais próxima?**
express (special delivery)	**expresso**
registered	**registrado**

PUBLIC TRANSPORTATION (*transporte público urbano*)

Buses (*autocarro*). Most of the island is covered by public buses, which are cheap, reliable, and generally punctual. For those with the luxury of time and patience, it's possible to go almost anywhere coach tours do by public bus — a much cheaper but more time-consuming alternative. Week-long tourist passes for orange town buses are available from bus ticket kiosks, where you may also buy roundtrip tickets. Otherwise you may purchase your ticket on the bus. Bus stops are indicated by the sign *paragem*.

The tourist office has a leaflet on bus services and routes. The two largest operators, SAM and Rodoeste, have bus stations in different locations. It's more convenient to catch SAM and Rodoeste buses at their main departure points on the Avenida do Mar e das Comunidades Madeirenses, either buying tickets on the bus itself or at the operators' kiosks near the bus departure points. Some intra-city and inter-city buses have identical bus numbers — for example, the orange town bus no. 20 that goes to Monte is not the same as the green/cream island bus no. 20 that goes to Santo da Serra.

Taxi. Metered taxis — which can be hailed in the street — are reasonably priced and convenient for most trips within Funchal and to sights just outside the city (such as Monte, the Botanic Garden, and the Quinta do Palheiro). For such trips, there is a government-set flat fare of 1,500 esc. one-way/3,000 esc. roundtrip. Otherwise, the meter begins at 300 esc. From downtown to the hotel zone, expect to pay about 700 esc. The rates are 20% higher after 10pm and on weekends and holidays.

Many people hire taxis as substitutes for coach tours to destinations around the island. If several people are traveling, this can be a good deal. (Most taxis will charge about 15,000 esc. a day.) A list of popular excursions and prices is kept at the tourist office.

Cable car. A brand new cable car, due to be completed in late 2000, connects Funchal to Monte, in the mountains above the city. The trip will take approximately 10 minutes from Funchal to Monte. There are plans for cable cars to be extended to Pico do Arieiro with a fantastic ride over the ecological park.

By air to Porto Santo. Porto Santo can be easily reached several times a day by small aircraft from the airport in Madeira directly to Porto Santo's new airport. Flight time is approximately 15 minutes and costs about 15,000 esc. roundtrip. Contract TAP at Tel. 291/239 210.

By Ferry to Porto Santo. The Porto Santo Line ferry leaves from the Funchal marina (Rua da Praia, 4; Tel. 291/210 300) daily at 8am, arriving in Porto Santo about 2 hours later. The return trip departs at 6pm. (In winter the timetable is usually slightly reduced.) Outside summer the crossing can be very rough (anti-seasickness pills are recommended).

Where can I get a taxi?	**Onde posso encontrar um táxi?**
What's the fare to ... ?	**Quanto custa um bilhete para ...?**
Where is the nearest bus stop?	**Onde é a paragem de auto-carros mais próxima?**
When's the next bus to ...?	**Quando parte o próximo autocarro para ...?**

Madeira

I want a ticket to ... single/return	**Queria um bilhete para ... ida/ida e volta**
Will you tell me when to get off?	**Pode dizer-me quando devo descer?**

R

RELIGION

The religion of Madeira, as in the rest of Portugal, is Roman Catholic. Besides Catholic churches in every small village, visitors will find surviving religious rituals and saints' days respected as public holidays.

Anglican Sunday services are conducted in Funchal's English Church on Rua da Quebra Costas, 18, and the Scottish Kirk (Church), at the corner of Rua do Conselheiro and Rua Ivens, has services on the first Sunday of each month. A Presbyterian church is found on Rua Consolado, 47. The tourist information office has a list of services for English-speaking Catholics, and other services.

T

TELEPHONE *(telefone)*

Portugal's country code is 351. The local area code, 291, must be dialed before all phone numbers, even for local calls (9-digit total). Note that prefixes changed in October 1999, and you may still see old numbers in print (i.e., "091" instead of "291").

White Portugal Telecom public telephones that accept both coins and prepaid telephone cards are found in Madeira. Coin boxes take 20, 50, and 100 esc. coins; unused coins are returned. *Credifone* telephone cards, a better option, can be purchased at post offices.

Local, national, and international calls can also be made from hotels, but almost always with an exorbitant surcharge. You are wise to make these with an international calling card, if you must make them from your hotel room. (Before departure, be sure to get the

international access code in Portugal for your long distance telephone carrier at home.)

   To call, pick up the receiver, insert card or coin, wait for the dial
tone, and dial. To make an international call, dial 00 for an international line + the country code (both Europe and overseas; eg UK
0044, US 001) + phone number (including the area code, without the
initial '0', where there is one). If you wish to send a fax, you may do
so from most hotels, though the charge may seem high.

   Dial 099 for the international operator for Europe, 098 for the rest
of the world. For directory inquiries within Madeira, dial 118.

reverse-charge call	**paga pelo destinatário**
Can you get me this number?	**Pode ligar-me para este número?**
reverse-charge (collect) call	**paga pelo destinatário**
person-to-person (personal) call	**com pré-aviso**

TIME ZONES (*hora local*)
Madeira operates both winter (GMT + 0) and summer (GMT + 1)
time periods. If traveling from Britain, do not adjust your watch as
Madeira is on the same time. From the last Sunday in March until
the last Sunday in October, the clocks are moved one hour ahead for
summer time.

Summer time chart.

Los Angeles	Chicago	New York	London	**Madeira**
4am	6am	7am	noon	**noon**

TIPPING (*serviço; gorjeta*)
Hotel and restaurant bills are generally all-inclusive, but an additional
tip of 5–10% is common and even expected in restaurants. Hotel porters,
per bag, generally receive 100 esc. Taxi drivers do not normally expect
a tip, though one should be given for any special services or information rendered. Hotel maids generally receive 100–200 esc. per day.

Madeira

TOILETS *(toilete; lavabo; quarto de banho; serviços)*
Public toilets in Funchal are few and far between, and not usually recommended. The best place to find a clean toilet is in a large hotel or a restaurant or bar. (In the latter, out of courtesy you should buy a drink, or at least ask permission.) "Ladies' is marked *Senhoras* and "Gents" *Homens* or *Senhores*. Be careful not to confuse *Senhoras* and *Senhores*!

Where are the toilets?   **¿Onde é o lavabo/quarto de banho?**

TOURIST INFORMATION *(oficina de turismo; informação turística)*
Portuguese National Tourist Offices (ICEP, or *Investimentos, Comércio e Turismo de Portugal*) are maintained in many countries:

Canada: Suite 1005, 60 Bloor Street West, Toronto, Ont. M4W 3B8; Tel. (416) 921 7376.

Ireland: 54 Dawson Street, Dublin. Tel. (353) 670 9133.

South Africa: 4th floor, Sunnyside Ridge, Sunnyside Drive. PO Box 2473 Houghton, Johannesburg. Tel. (2711) 484 3487.

UK: 22/25a Sackville St, London W1X 1DE; Tel. (071) 494 1441.

US: 590 Fifth Ave, 4th floor, New York, NY 10036; Tel. (212) 354 4403.

The Regional Department of Tourism in Madeira claims to have 10 offices. The tourist information office in Funchal, the most dependable (Tel. 291/225 658 or 291/229 057; e-mail <info@ madeiratourism.org>), is located at Av. Arriaga, 18. It's open Monday to Friday 9am–8pm; Saturday and Sunday 9am–6pm. The airport tourist office (Tel. 291/524 933) is open daily 9:30am–11:30pm.

Provincial offices — in Caniço, Machico, Ribeira Brava, Câmara de Lobos, Porto Moniz, Santana, and Porto Santo — keep normal business hours, though most close for lunch and a couple are not open in the afternoon. You can also get information on Madeira from the main tourist office in Lisbon (Palácio da Foz, Praça dos Restauradores; Tel. 21/346 91 13), open Monday–Friday 8am–7pm.

WEB SITES AND INTERNET CAFÉS

Web Sites

There are quite a few web sites that will assist you in getting information before you go. They include:

<www.madeira-island.com> A periodic webzine with events, chat room and links to travel providers, hotels, etc.

<www.madeira-web.com> Run by Madeira's Regional Tourism office, in English, German, and Norwegian, with a guide to outdoor activities, island tours, and real estate. Has live web camera and panorama movies

<www.madinfo.pt> An online database with information on cultural events, jobs, and more.

<www.madeiraonline.com> Has detailed information on and links to bargain flights to Madeira, lists of doctors and health services, the performing arts, sports and more, mostly in English.

<www.madeiraturismo.org> A helpful site with lots of information on hotels, restaurants, ecotourism and events.

<www.madeirawine.com> Information on local wines and an e-shop.

Also, try these general information sites on Portugal:

<www.portugal.org>

<www.travel.org/portugal>

<www.winesofportugal.org>

<www.portugal-live.net>

Internet Cafés

Cybercafe (Avenida do Infante, 6) charges a variable rate for computer use and Internet connection.

Madeira

WEIGHTS AND MEASURES

Length

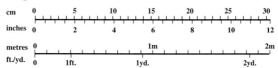

Weight

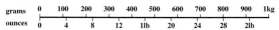

Temperature

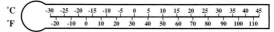

Fluid measures

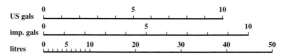

Distance

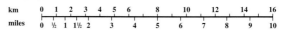

Y

YOUTH HOSTELS (*pousadas de juventude*)
There are, as of yet, no official youth hostels in Madeira or Porto
Santo. However, at a future date you can contact the Associação
Portuguesa de Pousadas de Juventude at Avenida Duque de Ávila
137, 1000 Lisbon; Tel. 21/355 90 81.

Recommended Hotels

Madeira's hotels, many of them traditional, older style accommodations, have long have been clustered in the hotel and tourist zones hugging Funchal's western coast. In recent years, many of those hotels have been urgently updating their design and services, as even more hotels are being built in the *zona turista*. At the same time, the hotel offerings across the island are rapidly being expanded, and visitors can now choose from hotels, *quintas* (villas), *estalagens* and *pousadas* (inns) along the coasts and in the villages and mountains of the interior.

Book especially early for Christmas and New Year's (when most hotels charge a huge supplement) and for smaller hotels throughout the year. Otherwise, high season rates generally apply February through May and late July to the end of September. Room price guidelines below are for a double room with bath in high season, including breakfast and VAT (value-added tax). All hotels accept major credit cards. For making reservations, Portugal's country code is 351; the prefix for Madeira is 291.

$$$$	Very Expensive (above 26,000 esc.)
$$$	Expensive (18,000–26,000 esc.)
$$	Moderate (12,000–17,000 esc.)
$	Inexpensive (below 12,000 esc.)

FUNCHAL HOTEL ZONE

Aparthotel Imperatriz $ *Rua Imperatriz Dona Amélia 72, 9000 Funchal; Tel. 291/233 456; fax 291/229 558.* Surrounded by upscale, luxury hotels, these reasonably equipped studio apartments, all with kitchenette and balcony, have a rooftop pool with views of the sea. A good economical choice. 27 studios.

Avenue Park Apartamentos Turísticos $$ *Avenido do Infante, 26, 9000 Funchal; Tel. 291/205 630; fax 291/205 659; e-mail <avenuePark@mail.telepac.pt>*.Opened in 1998, these smart apartments (studios and one- and two-bedrooms) are across from the Santa Catarina park and the casino, and just a 5-minute walk from downtown. Fashionably outfitted with modern furnishings in bright colors and nice, clean kitchenettes. Disabled access. 15 apartments.

Hotel Savoy $$$$ *Avenido do Infante, 9004 Funchal; Tel. 291/222 031; fax 291/223 103; <www.madinfo.pt/hotel/savoy>*. One of Madeira's great traditional hotels, the Savoy is virtually unrivaled for its personal service — one reason it has so many repeat visitors. The unprepossessing exterior belies the opulence of its public rooms. An outdoor pool terrace was built in the late 90s, and a new expansion will create luxurious apartments just beyond the gardens, right on the lido. Two synthetic-grass tennis courts, nightclub, three recommended restaurants, and excellent spa/indoor pool. Disabled access. 350 rooms.

Madeira Carlton $$$$ *Largo António Nobre, 9004 Funchal; Tel. 291/239 500; fax 291/223 337; <www.madinfo.pt/pestana>*. An attractive and luxurious complex that sits on a clifftop overlooking Funchal Bay. The hotel spans a river gorge adjacent to Reid's Hotel, with direct views of the ocean. Large, comfortable rooms, all with balconies. Four restaurants and lively nightlife, as well as tennis court, two swimming pools, and other sports facilities. Package deals available. Disabled access. 375 rooms.

Madeira Regency Club $$$ *Rua Carvalho Araújo, 9004 Funchal; Tel. 291/232 344; fax 291/232 374; <www.madeiraregency.net>*. Spacious and well-equipped poolside apartments with sun terraces and access to the sea. The staff are exceptionally friendly. Facilities include a sauna and squash courts. Disabled access. 96 rooms.

Pestana Carlton Park Resort & Casino $$$$ *Quinta da Vigia (Rua Imperatriz Dona Amélia), 9004 Funchal; Tel. 291/209 100; fax 291/232 076; e-mail <cph.reservas@pestana. org>.* This large, 60s-modern concrete complex (designed by Oscar Niemeyer) has a magnificent location, set within its own gardens overlooking the coast and harbor. It takes the resort part of its name seriously, with large pool, activities, and nightly entertainment at its adjacent casino and nightclubs. Slightly less expensive than competing 5-star hotels. Disabled access. 327 rooms.

Quinta Penha de França $–$$ *Rua da Penha de França, 9000 Funchal; Tel. 291/204 650; fax 291/229 261; <www. hotelquintapenhafranca.com>.* This *albergaria*, a restored manor house, is tucked away in a lovely garden in the midst of Funchal's hotel district. Though small and intimate, it nevertheless has a piano bar, outdoor dining, lawn and a swimming pool with an expansive terrace and terrific sea views. Stylish rooms. A new extension has been built down to sea level. Disabled access. 76 rooms.

Quinta Perestrelo $$$ *Rua Dr. Pita 3, 9000 Funchal; Tel. 291/762 333; fax 291/763 777; <www.charminghotelsmadeira. com>.* A charming, 150-year-old country house with period antiques, a lovely garden and swimming pool. Close to Quinta Magnolia park, but adjacent to a busy road junction. 30 rooms.

Reid's Palace $$$$ *Estrada Monumental 139; Tel. 291/71 71 71 (in US: 201/265-5151; toll-free in UK: 800 092 1723); fax 291/71 71 77; <www.reidspalace.orient-express.com>.* Madeira's legendary hotel — *the* place for the English abroad — is a magnificent mansion that preserves the elegance of another era. Sumptuously redecorated in mid-'90s. The hotel has magnificent gardens overlooking the sea, spacious sun terraces, swimming pools, and tennis courts. Ask about a wide variety of packages, some surprisingly affordable. Disabled access. 173 rooms.

The Cliff Bay Hotel $$$$ *Estrada Monumental, 147, 9000 Funchal; Tel. 291/707 700 (toll-free in UK: 0800 964-328; toll-free in Germany, 013081 9477); fax 291/762 524; <www. portobay.com>.* A luxurious hotel, one of the more recent additions to the hotel zone, that sits on a bluff and has panoramic sea and harbor views from nearly all its rooms. It pampers guests with large, fashionable rooms; spacious and well-equipped bathrooms; and excellent facilities, including two pools, health club, tennis court and choice of restaurants. Disabled access. 201 rooms.

FUNCHAL TOURIST ZONE

Madeira Palácio $$$ *Estrada Monumental, 265, 9000 Funchal; Tel. 291/702 701; fax 291/764 478; <www.madinfo.pt/ hotel/mpalacio>.* One of the old-time favorites in Madeira, this traditional hotel is struggling to keep pace with its 5-star neighbors. It has attractive grounds, good views, tennis courts and a nice pool. Plans for a late-2000 renovation of the lobby, which will give it a colonial appearance, and addition of an indoor pool are very welcome. Disabled access. 253 rooms.

Carlton Village Resort Hotel $$$ *Estrada Monumental 194, 9000 Funchal; Tel. 291/701 600; fax 291/763 988; e-mail <village@pestana.org>.* Looking like a well-designed village straight out of a Mexican resort, the Village Hotel has a faux Moorish lobby and beautifully landscaped pool area and gardens. Nicely equipped studio apartment suites and a relaxing spa center. Half-board available. Disabled access. 200 rooms.

Crowne Plaza Resort Madeira $$$$ *Estrada Monumental 175-177, 9000 Funchal; Tel. 291/717 700; fax 291/717 71; <www.crowneplaza.com>.* The newest five-star member of the tourist zone (opened February 2000) is by far the most modern. A pair of ultra-sleek behemoth buildings line the coast. The décor inside is just as minimalist and swank, and all rooms have panoramic ocean views. Guests have little reason to leave: there are four restaurants, an Irish pub, two indoor and two outdoor pools, spa, tennis and squash courts, diving center, and more. Disabled access. 300 rooms.

Eden Mar Suite Hotel $$$ *Rua do Gorgulho 2, 9004 Funchal; Tel. 291/762 221; fax 291/761 966; <www. eden-mar.com>.* A well-equipped, popular, and modern aparthotel set in a busy location in the heart of the tourist zone. All studios have kitchenette, private balcony, and sea views. Facilities include outdoor and indoor pools, health club and sauna, sun terrace with a pleasant garden, and restaurant. Free transport to Palheiro Golf and special offers for week-long stays. Disabled access. 146 rooms.

Hotel Girassol $$$ *Estrada Monumental 256, 9000 Funchal; Tel. 291/764 051; fax 291/765 441.* A modern hotel, pleasant and friendly, with a consistent package business. Rooms are basic, but many have excellent sea views. Though located on the busy main Funchal highway, it features a secluded garden and swimming pool. Disabled access. 133 rooms.

Carlton Palms $$$ *Rua do Gorgulho 17, 9000 Funchal; Tel. 291/766 100; fax 291/766 247.* On the seafront, this newish aparthotel incorporates a refurbished *quinta*. All rooms are nicely furnished, self-catering studios. Heated swimming pool, health club, gymnasium. 167 rooms.

Ocean Park Resort Hotel $$$$ *Estrada Monumental, 9000 Funchal; Tel. 291/702 000; fax 291/702 020; <www. dorisol.pt>.* Another of the big and bold 5-star hotels to sprout along the coast in the tourist zone, the Ocean Park competes with the Crowne Plaza to see which offers more of everything. It is awash in sports, facilities, and services, and the modern rooms are plush. Disabled access. 349 rooms.

Pensão Vila Vicência $ *Caminho Velho da Ajuda 45, 9000 Funchal; Tel. 291/771 527; fax: 291/771 538.* A charming, family-run pension comprising three adjacent houses, Vila Vicência is just a 5-minute walk from the Lido complex. It has a lovely small garden with a private swimming pool. 30 rooms.

FUNCHAL TOWN

Hotel Porto Santa Maria $$$ *Avenida do Mar e das Comunidades Madeirenses 50, 9050 Funchal; Tel. 291/206 700; fax 291/206 720; <www.portosantamaria.com>.* Opening in late 2000, this new hotel is named for a nearby street in the historic center of Funchal. Next to the 17th-century São Tiago fortress, and owned by the group that includes the luxurious Cliff Bay, it overlooks the ocean and is designed to evoke the Mediterranean. Rooms are modern, and studio apartments are available. Disabled access. 147 rooms.

Castanheiro $ *Rua do Castanheiro 27, 9000 Funchal; Tel. 291/227 060; fax 291/227 940.* Good-value apartments in an excellent location just off Praça do Município. Well-equipped rooms, friendly staff, and recommended snack-bar restaurant adjacent. 32 apartments.

Windsor Hotel $$ *Rua das Hortas 4, 9000 Funchal; Tel. 291/233 083; fax 291/233 080.* A modern hotel right in the busy center of Funchal, the Windsor has rather plain rooms without views, but good facilities and service, and a very nice rooftop pool and terrace. Very convenient and inexpensive. Disabled access. 67 rooms.

Hotel Santa Maria $ *Rua João de Deus 26, 9000 Funchal. Tel. 291/225 271; fax 291/221 542.* A simple hotel in the center of town, not far from the municipal market; not without its charms — namely its rooftop pool with views of all Funchal, and its economical price. 83 rooms.

BEYOND FUNCHAL

Casa das Videiras $ *Sítio Serra d'Água, 9270 Seixal; Tel. 291/854 020; fax 291/854 021; <www.casa-das-videiras.com>.* A charming guesthouse in a tiny, pretty town on the north coast. The mid-19th-century manor house has clean and charmingly decorated rooms, and the atmosphere is very friendly and relaxed, a tribute to the hands-on owner. Self-catering possible. Deals available: stay 7 nights, pay 6; stay 14 nights, pay 12. 4 rooms.

Casa do Caseiro $ *Caminho do Monte, 62, 9050 Funchal; Tel. 291/759 025; fax 291/227 113.* Set high above Funchal, halfway down the Monte toboggan run, this charming and private small house has been sympathetically restored and comes with use of its small swimming pool. Attractive gardens and terrace. 7 rooms.

Dom Pedro Baía $$–$$$ *Estrada de São Roque, 9200 Machico. Tel. 291/969 500; fax 291/969 501; <www. dompedro.com>.* A modern high-rise overlooking the bay of Machico, Madeira's first settlement, this comfortable hotel is a good base for exploring the eastern third of the island. Popular with British and German packagers, it has an Olympic-size swimming pool, tennis court, bar, and nightly entertainment. Disabled access. 218 rooms.

Estalagem Casa Velha do Palheiro (Palheiro Golf)
$$$$ *Palheiro Golf, São Gonçalo, 9050 Funchal. Tel. 291/794 901; fax 291/794 925; <www.casa-velha.com>.* Nestled in the hills east of Funchal, with great views of the city, this handsome and stylish inn occupies a beautiful 1804 country estate house connected to the Quinta do Palheiro — the most magnificent private gardens in Madeira. Luxuriously decorated rooms. Open only since 1997, it's part of the esteemed Palheiro Golf Club (special golf packages available) — the only hotel in Madeira on a golf course — and has an elegant restaurant, heated swimming pool, gym, and tennis court. 37 rooms.

Estalagem Eira do Serrado $$–$$$ *Eira do Serrado, Curral das Freiras; Tel. (mobil) 0936/601 37 52.* At press time, this inn, planned as a 4-star guesthouse with elegant rooms, all with balconies, had yet to be built. But the setting is so splendid — at the lookout point (1095 m/3592 ft) overlooking a valley of green terraces and the isolated village of Curral das Freiras — that you may want to check in when you inevitably visit Eira do Serrado. Game room, restaurant, Jacuzzi and sauna, and wine cellar. 25 rooms.

Estalagem do Mar $ *Juncos, Fajã Da Areia, São Vicente. Tel. 291/840 010; fax 291/840 019; e-mail <estalagem. mar@mail.telepac.pt>.* Within walking distance of São Vicente, and sandwiched between a sheer cliff and the roaring sea, this sprawling hotel buys exclusivity at a bargain price. All the rooms, simply furnished, face the ocean. Indoor and outdoor pool, restaurant, and tennis court.

Estalagem Quinta do Estreito $$$$ *Rua José Joaquim da Costa, 9532 Estreito de Câmara de Lobos; Tel. 291/910 530; fax 291/910 549; <www.charminghotelsmadeira.com/q-estreito>.*

A luxury *quinta*, or villa, with elegant furnishings set 400 m (437 ft) above sea level, overlooking the vineyards of *Câmara de Lobos*. A relaxing hideaway, it has landscaped tropical gardens, restaurant, library, and heated pool. Warm and tastefully decorated rooms. 48 rooms.

Pousada dos Vinháticos $$ *Serra de Água, 9350 Ribeira Brava. Tel. 291/70 20 30; fax 291/70 20 20; <www.dorisol.pt>.* This chalet-style inn — owned by a hotel group, not the Portuguese government as are the *pousadas* on the mainland — is a terrific mountain refuge. Ideal for nature enthusiasts and those in search of serenity, the inn has a splendid new addition, a wood-cabin lodge with unmatched views and extremely comfortable rooms. Excellent restaurant, game room, and very friendly staff. 21 rooms.

Pousada do Pico do Arieiro $$$ *Pico do Ariero, 9006 Funchal Codex. Tel.291/230 110; fax 291/228 611; <www. dorisol.pt>.* A modern, unassuming lodge where there's little else — on top of Madeira's second-highest peak. Only a decade old, but it's aged considerably. The big draws are the strenuous hike to Pico do Ruivo and the privilege of being able to wake up on a dramatic, moon-like mountaintop. Predictably, a favorite with trekkers. Good restaurant. 18 rooms.

Pousada de Santo Antão $ *Seixal. Tel.291/854 210; fax 291/854 212; <www.dorisol.pt>.* A five-bedroom village house in the attractive village of Seixal, on the north coast. This comfortable inn is the property of the company that runs two other rustic mountain lodges (*pousadas*). A good deal. 5 rooms.

Quinta da Bela Vista $$$$ *Caminho do Avista Navios 4, 9000 Funchal; Tel. 291/764 144; fax 291/765 090.* A swank, 150-year old family-run hotel 3 km (2 miles) west of Funchal with splendid views and a lovely garden. Beautiful rooms with antiques, excellent food at the formal restaurant. Small gym and sauna, swimming pool, library. 67 rooms.

Quinta do Furão $$ *Achada do Gramacho, Santana. Tel. 291/57 01 00; fax 291/57 21 31; e-mail <quintadofurao@ hotmail.com>*. A rural chalet-like inn with astounding views of the rugged north coast and the undulating green hills around Santana, this estate (named for non-existent ferrets) offers style and relaxation surrounded by orchards and a vineyard. Walking trails, a cool little pool with a retractable roof, and a fine rustic restaurant. 43 rooms.

Residencial Amparo $ *Rua da Amargura, Machico. Tel. 291/968 120; fax 291/960 050*. A simple hotel, comfortably decorated, in the center of Machico, just two blocks from the pebbly beach. A pleasant and personal alternative to the larger and more institutional Dom Pedro. Attractive restaurant. 12 rooms.

Residencial Encumeada $ *Feiteiras, Serra d'Água. Tel. 291/951 282; fax 291/951 281*. Few places can match the setting of this unpretentious lodging, which has been expanded. Just down the road from the Encumeada pass, the hotel sits on a ledge overlooking the mountains and valley around Serra de Água, halfway between the north and south coasts. Ideal for walkers and hikers. 50 rooms.

PORTO SANTO

Torre Praia Suite Hotel $$$ *Rua Goulart Medeiros, 9400 Porto Santo. Tel. 291/985 292; fax 291/982 487*. Just outside Vila Baleira, this attractive 4-star beach hotel has simple furnishings and overlooks Porto Santo's excellent beach and the ocean. Kidney-shaped swimming pool, squash court, gym, sauna and Jacuzzi, game room. 65 rooms.

Recommended Restaurants

Dining in Madeira for most visitors used to be limited to hotels and the odd café or snack bar encountered in Funchal or wherever their coach stopped for lunch during an all-day tour. The restaurant scene, however, is improving and catering to a more diverse clientele, and while some of the finest restaurants on the island are still found in the top hotels, there is now a wider variety than ever.

Restaurants known as *típicos* are basic eateries (often rustic, or at least decorated in a rustic style), where the menu is often limited to Madeiran dishes (*pratos típicos*). A good *típico* is worth a detour, but some of these have been spoiled by a constant stream of coach and cruise passengers; they seem far more intent on separating tourists from their escudos than offering genuine Madeiran food.

The prices indicated are for starter, main course and dessert, with wine, per person. (Note that some fish or shellfish dishes will be more expensive.) Service and VAT of 16% are included, as they generally are in the bill. Except where noted, all restaurants accept major credit cards.

Prices normally include taxes and a service charge, but it is customary to leave an additional 5-10% tip for good service.

$$$$	Very Expensive (over 7,000 esc.)
$$$	Expensive (4,000-7,000 esc.)
$$	Moderate (2,500-4,000 esc.)
$	Inexpensive (below 2,500 esc.)

FUNCHAL TOWN

Carochina $–$$ *Rua São Francisco, 2A; Tel. 291/223 695. Open Tues–Sat for lunch and dinner.* Catering to British vacationers, this small, candlelit restaurant opposite the city park serves English and international home-cooked cuisine. A good bet if you've had your fill of Madeiran and Portuguese cooking.

Golden Gate Grand Café $–$$ *Avenida Arriaga, 29; Tel. 291/234 383. Open daily for lunch and dinner.* This attractive café, in a 19th-century colonial-style house on the main street opposite the São Francisco wine lodge, is a great spot. Choose from a light menu downstairs, or a full menu upstairs in the attractive, airy restaurant. Live music most nights.

O Celeiro $$–$$$ *Rua dos Aranhas, 22; Tel. 291/230 622. Open daily for lunch and dinner.* This highly-rated, rustic cellar restaurant is popular with both locals and foreign visitors. Fresh fish, *espetadas* (kebabs) and *cataplana* are among the house specialties. Good wine list.

Restaurant Caravela $$$ *Avenida das Comunidades Madeirenses, 15 (3rd floor). Tel. 291/228 464. Open daily for lunch and dinner.* In the city center, this 30-year-old restaurant remains fashionable for its panoramic views of sea and Portuguese cuisine focusing on fresh fish and shellfish. There's a glass-enclosed terrace as well as an inner dining room.

FUNCHAL HOTEL ZONE

Casa dos Reis $$$ *Rua Imperatriz Dona Amélia, 101; Tel. 291/225 182. Open daily for dinner.* An attractive and small, formal restaurant, serving a wide range of international, French, and Portuguese dishes. Try the charcoal-grilled lamb or scabbard fish, an island specialty, with green pepper sauce.

Casa Velha $$$ *Rua Imperatriz Dona Amélia, 69; Tel. 291/205 600. Open daily for lunch and dinner.* A formal garden-like restaurant with bamboo chairs, ferns, and ceiling fans, the "Old House" has a 19th-century colonial feel. The short international and Madeiran menu is popular with nearby hotel guests. Try *espada flambé* (scabbard fish) with champagne. Piano bar downstairs.

Dona Amélia $$–$$$ *Rua Imperatriz Dona Amélia, 83; Tel. 291/225 784. Open daily for lunch and dinner.* This chic upstairs restaurant behind the Savoy hotel is a good place for a romantic dinner of *espetadas* (kebabs), grilled fish, nice salads, and soups.

Fleur de Lys $$$$ *Avenida do Infante (in Savoy Hotel); Tel. 291/223 031. Open daily for dinner.* The Savoy Hotel's entry in the luxury dining category is a standout. It has spectacular panoramic views and Old World elegance and service. The French menu, overseen by a Michelin-starred chef, is meticulously prepared and presented.

Joe's Bar $–$$ *Rua da Penha de França; Tel. 291/229 087. Open daily for lunch and dinner.* Eat on the attractive garden terraces or in an attractive dining room. Check out the chalkboard menu outside, which includes a dish of the day, often a fresh fish course.

Kon Tiki $$ *Rua do Favila, 9; Tel. 291/764 737. Open daily for lunch and dinner.* Offering an interesting menu of Madeiran favorites with an international twist, such as shark steak and *espada* with prawns flambé, as well as specialties from Finland (fillet steak prepared on a hot stone).

Les Faunes $$$$ *Estrada Monumental, 139 (in Reid's Palace Hotel); Tel. 291/763 001. Open daily for dinner (closed April–October).* Reid's elegant winter restaurant is something special — enough so that many diners wear black-tie. The standard-bearer on Madeira for haute cuisine, this elegant dining room overlooking the harbor is the place for refined ambience with piano accompaniment.

Quinta Palmeira $$$–$$$$ *Avenida do Infante, 5; Tel. 291/221 814. Open daily for lunch and dinner.* One of Madeira's finest restaurants, this handsome 18th-century townhouse (next to the Savoy Hotel) has an elegantly appointed dining room and terrace for relaxed, open-air dining. Many terrific dishes, including smoked swordfish wrapped around hearts of palm and served with caviar, and *espada* (scabbard fish) with bananas and passion-fruit sauce. Excellent wine list and attentive service.

FUNCHAL TOURIST ZONE

Casa Madeirense $$$ *Estrada Monumental, 153; Tel. 291/766 700. Open Mon–Sat for lunch and dinner.* Sandwiched in the midst of the tourist zone's biggest and best five-star hotels, this comfortable restaurant could be Madeira's entry in the World Expo: it nearly goes overboard with regional gastronomy and folklore (the bar is made to look like a *palheiro*, typical A-frame house of Santana). But it's a popular place, good for sampling *cataplana de mariscos* and other seafood dishes.

Restaurante Tokos $$$ *Estrada Monumental, 169; Tel. 291/771 019. Open Tues–Sun for lunch and dinner.* A tiny, personal restaurant with an eccentric chef/owner, this intimate place (just 10 or so tables) does everything well, but when the chef wheels out the cart of fresh fish for you to choose from, you'll be hard-pressed to order anything else. Fresh vegetables, excellent desserts, and a very good wine cellar. Reservations essential.

Trattoria Villa Cliff $$$ *Estrada Monumental, 139; Tel. 291/717 100. Open daily for lunch and dinner.* Just down the road from Reid's Palace, this handsome Italian restaurant (owned by Reid's) serves excellent pastas, fish, and meat dishes, complemented by a terrific wine list. Have a cocktail at the bar and wait for table on the terrace.

Tropical $$$ *Estrada Monumental, 306 (in Hotel Florasol); Tel. 219/700 840. Open daily.* One of Funchal's most popular restaurants, with an international-Madeiran menu famous for its *flambé* desserts. Live music and a boisterous crowd nightly.

BEYOND FUNCHAL

Casa Velha do Palheiro $$$$ *Palheiro Golf, São Gonçalo (Funchal). Tel. 291/794 901. Open daily for lunch and dinner.* One of the island's most elegant restaurants is the refined dining room on the grounds of the Quinta do Palheiro about 3 km east of Funchal. Exquisite French and Portuguese dishes. Daily prix-fixe and à la carte menu. Superb service and wine list.

Estalagem do Mar $ *Juncos, Fajâ Da Areia, São Vicente. Tel. 291/840 010. Open daily for lunch and dinner.* A popular hotel restaurant with panoramic views of the ocean. Both hotel guests and visitors can be assured of a dependable, reasonably priced meal of fresh seafood, including swordfish and sea bass.

Restaurante Cachalote $$ *Ilhéumar (Porto Moniz); Tel. 291/853 180. Open daily for lunch and dinner.* This restaurant, perched on the rocks near the natural pools of Porto Moniz on the north coast, does a brisk daytime coach tour business. Madeiran specialties and tidily prepared seafood dishes take a backseat to the stupendous panoramic ocean views from two floors.

Pousada do Pico do Arieiro $$$ *Pico do Ariero; Tel. 291/230 110; fax 291/228 611; Open daily for lunch and dinner.* There's nowhere else to eat on top of Madeira's second-highest peak, so it's good news that this pousada restaurant serves well-prepared, hearty Portuguese dishes such as pepper steak and rack of lamb, that will satisfy mountain trekkers. The glassed-in restaurant has unequaled views of the rugged terrain.

Madeira

Pousada dos Vinháticos $$–$$$ *Serra de Água. Tel. 291/70 20 30; Open daily for lunch and dinner.* This chalet-style inn has an excellent restaurant with panoramic views of the surrounding mountains. It serves mostly Madeiran and Portuguese specialties, but does an excellent Chateaubriand for two. Nice wine list and friendly service. Downstairs bar and outdoor terrace.

Quinta do Furão $$ *Achada do Gramacho, Santana. Tel. 291/57 01 00; Open daily for lunch and dinner.* This rustic restaurant, part of the recommended hotel of the same name, serves some of the finest food on the entire north coast. Surrounded by orchards and a vineyard, it offers the freshest of local ingredients and seafood.

Santo António $ *Estreito-Câmara de Lobos; Tel. 291/945 439. Open daily for lunch and dinner.* A simple, friendly, and bustling restaurant, ideal for lunch. *Espetada* (meat or fish skewers) is the most popular pick of a short menu.

Victor's Bar $$ *Ribeiro Frio; Tel. 291/575 898. Open daily for lunch and dinner.* A cozy bar reminiscent of an English pub leads to a chalet-like dining area with a fireplace. Grilled trout, plucked fresh from the hatchery across the road, is the house specialty.

PORTO SANTO

Teodorico $ *Sera de Fora; Tel. 291/984 425. Open daily for lunch and dinner.* The place in Porto Santo to get *espetada* — grilled beef served on a skewer, an island specialty — is this comfortable onetime farmhouse, popular with locals and visitors. Although there are other dishes on the menu, virtually everyone orders the *espetada*, which is served with vegetables, potatoes, and excellent Madeiran bread, *pão de caco*. Outdoor seating. No credit cards.

INDEX